Roy

All the best,

Richard Daft

On a Pedestal

Neil

9 October 2008

Neil Jenkinson

With a foreword by Lord Butler

First published in Great Britain by
Association of Cricket Statisticians and Historians
Cardiff CF11 9XR
© ACS, 2008

British Library Cataloguing-in-Publication Data.
A catalogue record for this book is available from the British
Library.

ISBN: 978 1 905138 64 7
Typeset by Limlow Books

Contents

Richard Daft in his fifties:
a portrait by an unknown artist

'The surname DAFT has been known in Nottingham since the thirteenth century: its significance is gentle.'

F.S.Ashley-Cooper, *A Cricketer's Yarns*, Chapman and Hall, 1926

'DAFT: English nickname for a meek person, rather than a stupid one: from Middle English – mild, gentle, meek. Old English – gedœfte. The surname survives in the East Midlands, in spite of the unfavourable connotations that were acquired by the word in the fifteenth century.'

Patrick Hanks and Flavia Hodges, *A Dictionary of Surnames*, Oxford University Press, 1988

Foreword

By the Rt Hon The Lord Butler, KG, GCB, CVO

My father was christened Bernard Daft Butler, being the son of Richard's daughter, Anne Huskinson Daft, by her second marriage. My father was sensitive about having 'Daft' as his middle name. In fact, it was the only thing about which I ever knew he told me an untruth. I remember asking him, as a small boy, what the 'D' stood for; and he told me 'Douglas'. I only discovered some years later that it really stood for 'Daft' and that Richard Daft had been one of the greatest cricketers of the second half of the nineteenth century.

I suppose that my father's sensitivity was understandable. By the time he was born in 1907, Richard Daft had been dead for seven years and the days of his cricketing glory had ended some sixteen years before. In Lancashire, where my father grew up, the word 'daft' had lost its East Midlands meaning of a meek or gentle person and definitely meant one apple short of a picnic. I can imagine my father would not have wanted his school companions in the playground to know that his middle name was 'Daft'.

By the time I discovered the truth, I was a sports-mad, and particularly cricket-mad, teenager. When I found out my father was the grandson of Richard and I was Richard Daft's great-grandson, I was thrilled to bits. I felt that if I had borne the great man's name, I would have blazoned it to the heavens. Much later on, Prime Minister John Major did it for me: whenever my name was mentioned, John never referred to me as Secretary of the Cabinet or Head of the Civil Service, but as Richard Daft's descendant. To tell the truth, I preferred it that way.

There may have been other reasons for my father's reticence. As Neil Jenkinson's biography makes clear, Richard Daft's life story has its low points as well as its high ones. Towards the end he was declared bankrupt, and in my father's time bankruptcy carried a greater stigma than it does today. Moreover, Anne Daft's first marriage, which took place in the year before her father died, ended quietly in divorce; and that too was a source of shame in the earlier years of the twentieth century. So my father may have regarded these as skeletons in the family's cupboard, whose bones he did not wish to shake.

Yet for all the disappointments of the latter part of his life, it was clear that my great-grandfather was a fine man. Despite growing up in very poor circumstances, he had a natural dignity and sufficient presence to be able to carry himself well on public occasions. He had a taste, and a prodigious talent, for a wide range of manly games and he seems to have played them honourably – indeed, more scrupulously than the man who came to overshadow him in the Victorian history of English cricket, W.G.Grace.

In 2007, the local History Society in Richard's home of Radcliffe-on-Trent, raised funds for the restoration of his grave in the local churchyard and, with my two cousins who are also Daft's great-grandchildren, I attended the re-dedication.

As I stood before Richard Daft's grave, a cricket ball's throw one side from the Manor House where he lodged with his future father-in-law, Butler Parr, on the other side from the brewery which he managed and the house in which he passed his married life, I had a strong sense of the man. I felt that I had been right, as a star-struck teenager, to be proud that he was my ancestor; and, as I have read Neil Jenkinson's account of him, which brings to life so vividly his story in the context of the other great Victorian cricketers with whom he played and whose names have become household words in cricket history, I feel it even more strongly. I am glad that Richard Daft's story has been written and I hope that other readers will enjoy it as much as I have done.

Chapter One
Nottingham, Queen of the Midlands

Geographical characteristics set Nottingham apart from its Midland neighbours. Twin peaks lying a mile west of the River Trent stand out above the flood plain. On one stands Nottingham Castle and on the other is the wonderful perpendicular building of St. Mary's, the mother church of the city. The lower-lying terrain between them was built upon long ago. In the early part of the nineteenth century, the town was a dirty and dangerous place. Noisy, smelly courtyards provided a pump and a midden, often conveniently placed adjacent to each other, to serve dozens of families. Human and animal effluent – the enormous cattle market remained bang in the town centre – was collected in carts and dumped near the River Trent, where it was used as fertiliser for the market gardens which lay near its banks. Cholera was an ever-present threat. The worst conditions were to improve after the mid-nineteenth century, but this was the town into which Richard Daft was born. He was lucky to see the light on the very northern fringe, in North Street, on 2 November, 1835. Richard was the youngest of four surviving sons of John and Sarah Daft: three others had died in infancy.

There are indications that Sarah Daft had married beneath her. Her brother, Thomas Wood, died a wealthy man, yet could not put a name to her family when he made his will, which suggests a prolonged estrangement between brother and sister. John Daft was not much of a catch as a husband. In the second volume of Richard Daft's reminiscences, *A Cricketer's Yarns*, published in 1926, Richard's eldest son, Richard Parr Daft, supplied details of the family's history. John Daft is presented as someone who, if not a hero, was a man of action who ran away and enlisted in the army and served in the cavalry under Wellington in Spain during the time of the Napoleonic war in the early 1800s. The reality is different. The only record in the national archive at Kew of a soldier named John Daft is found among the documents of the 69th Regiment of Foot. He was in the infantry, not the cavalry. John Daft enlisted at Nottingham in 1796 and, after an interval, re-enlisted there on 13 October, 1806 when he was already 45 years old, and served up to 13 September, 1817 before being sent home prior to his discharge.

John's journey home took as long as eleven months: he was not returning from Spain, for his military service took place almost entirely in India, or on the seas around it. In 1797, he was at sea when the Regiment was in training to prepare for battle against Napoleon's numerous agents in India. In 1805, the Regiment was in Malta, presumably returning to service in India: there ensued the astonishingly long period of eleven years while they were stationed in or around the sub-continent, with the objective of opposing Britain's French enemies and their associates among the local population.

Trichinopoly was their base until 1808; then they returned to Madras. For two years they were at sea. Eventually, by November 1816, they were back in India, at Bangalore. There, in September the following year, John Daft was given his discharge 'in consequence of old age and inability'. It cannot be said that serving in the heat of turbulent India or under sail in wooden warships for all that time was a safe and comfortable experience; he and his colleagues must have earned every penny of their meagre wages. Service under the great Duke's command was quite feasible for John Daft because, as Colonel Arthur Wellesley, Wellington pursued a victorious course against those Indian potentates who were hostile to British interests. By 1803, Britain had become the undisputed military power in India.

So John Daft was never in the Peninsula. He did not receive an heroic character reference; indeed, the certifying officer wrote: 'His general conduct has not been uniformly good, from an almost constant habit of drunkenness and other insubordinate acts.' The certificate of discharge describes him as about 53 years of age, five feet six inches in height, brown hair, dark eyes, dark complexion, and by trade a framework knitter.

Richard's baptismal certificate contains the same occupation; by that time, 1835, according to the certificate of discharge, John was 70 years old. Ashley-Cooper, on information received from Richard Parr Daft, says in *A Cricketer's Yarns* that he died at the age of 86, which might have been in 1851. On his marriage certificate, Richard describes his father as a glove maker. He surely must have expired by 1862. In all other documents he is referred to as a framework knitter, given the customary abbreviation 'fwk'. Richard's elder surviving siblings were Thomas, born 1817; John Henry, born 1823; and Charles Frederick, born 1830. North Street, Richard's first home, ran westward from Milton Street, along the south side of what is now Trinity Square. There was one way in which the area was privileged – it was right on the northern edge of town, with open space on the far side of North Street which is difficult to imagine now. The home of an ageing framework knitter could hardly be a prosperous one: most of the ground floor was taken up with the frame, where John Daft knitted stockings and other woollen garments. The knitter or one of the older children collected the woollen yarn from the warehouse. As Giles Worsley wrote about Victorian working-class homes, what cannot be replicated in our times is 'the dirt and damp, the smell of urine, and the oppressive sense of overcrowding that must have come from so many people living in such proximity.'

By 1841, young Richard was living with his family at Knotted Alley, which lay just north of the Nottingham Canal and the Midland Railway. Long ago destroyed by redevelopment, it cannot have been the most salubrious part of town, being highly susceptible to flooding, but may have been closer to the warehouses from which the wool awaited collection. The 1841 census records that John, whose age was given as 55, though he may have been rather older, and Sarah, 45, were living with three of their sons, John, aged 18, Charles, 11, and Richard, five.

Ten years later, the family had split up following the death of Richard's mother. His father was then living with a sister and her family in Sneinton, Nottingham, but Richard had left the town and was apprenticed to H.H.Greenwood at 9 Lowgate in the parish of St Mary's, Kingston-upon-Hull. The period of training, learning the characteristics of many different types of materials, running errands and living in, would have been a lengthy one. H.G.Wells, too was apprenticed in the trade and he acquired many of the attributes of a gentleman. This period of Richard's life must have had some considerable influence on his manner and personality. Though he did not care to mention it later, it contributed towards his becoming a man of some education, deemed suitable at the age of 26 to marry his boss's daughter and capable of running two businesses in tandem for many years.

Very early in his career, he was invited, as a young amateur, to play in country-house cricket for teams raised by the Earl of Stamford at Boston, Lincolnshire, and for Irnham Park near Bourne, against such distinguished opponents as the Old Harrovians. Later, as a parent, he showed that he appreciated the advantages of a private education by sending his sons to Trent College, the public school at Long Eaton in Derbyshire, just over the Nottinghamshire border. In 1879, when he led a side of professional cricketers on tour in Canada, the Governor-General, the Marquess of Lorne, and his wife, Queen Victoria's daughter, Princess Louise, were happy to engage in conversation with him.

Lord Harris, fifteen years his junior, refers to his most superior way of speech. Jimmy Catton, a well-known journalist for over fifty years, who knew Richard from the 1880s, says that he was called 'Dapper Richard Daft' but adds that 'Daft was quite a polished man of the world. Nature designed him for a country gentleman, for he had the tastes, the inclinations, the manners and the mode of speech of one who had received some education.' Elsewhere, he was described as 'lordly'. Only Daft among professionals would have asked Lord Harris, fielding at point, to desist from sledging while he, Daft, was batting.

In addition to his apprenticeship we can look to his mother and her family as an important influence. The little we know about them is based mainly on the career of her brother, Thomas Wood. His day job was that of a commercial traveller, operating on a big scale, from bases in Huddersfield, where he lived, and Nottingham, though his travels also took him to Scotland on behalf of his employers, woollen and worsted manufacturers. He also had a profitable sideline as investor in a big way in stocks and shares. He must have been a man of judgement to have accumulated wealth and to have kept it during the decline in share values in the early 1850s, which followed the exaggerated period of railway mania.

Chapter Two

Advancement in Life

The sons of John Daft may not even have heard of Thomas Wood, and the circumstances in which he came to their attention were sensational. In 1854, he was in his sixty-eighth year. At the end of November, while in Glasgow on business, he was taken ill. He must have had a premonition of disaster and, anxious to put his affairs in order, called for a lawyer. He was fortunate enough to find a good one in William Steele. He and his clerk, John Girvan, hastened to Wood's lodging, where they found that their client was a very sick man indeed. The circumstances were complex. Wood was, it appeared, extremely rich; he was far from his Huddersfield home, and he had no direct dependants, his nearest and dearest consisting of a large number of nieces and nephews who were the offspring of his two brothers and his sister.

When he came to the children of his sister Sarah, he was stretched to find a means of identifying them. He did not know how many children she had, but nephew William would because they all lived in Nottingham. Thomas' wish was that his nieces and nephews, who numbered eleven in all, should share equally in his fortune. To begin with, they would share only the income: the estate should be accumulated for the next generation.

At last, after hours of concentrated work, they finished the will and Steele read the contents to his client who scratched a feeble signature. Later that day, Thomas died. When the executors obtained Probate of the will, the value of his estate came to £24,000, or in present day values £1,786,560. In terms just of income at, say, five per cent, each might receive an annual income of around £8,000 on equivalent figures today.

For Richard, aged just 19, everything was changed. He was in a position to make changes in his lifestyle: he soon opted for the life of a country gentleman.

* * * * *

By the end of 1853, he had made his first recorded appearance in local cricket. The *Nottingham Review* of 29 July, 1853 records Nottingham Britannia Club 20 and 76 (R.Daft 0 and 36): Ilkeston Britannia Club 28 and 71 for seven, to win by three wickets.

This was a memorable start for the seventeen-year-old. Yet, after Richard's single reported appearance in July 1853, which ought to have ensured a further trial for Nottingham Britannia, he does not appear again for nearly three years. This was almost certainly due to his absence in Hull. He was already a rich young man when, in 1856, the *Nottingham Review* gave him an honourable mention but the comment, 'Mr. Daft, a very promising young cricketer, scored 30 . . .' sounds more like the introduction of an unknown player than a reference to an already familiar personality.

He turned out on 23 and 24 June for Notts Amateurs against Burton-on-Trent at Trent Bridge. A week later, on the same ground, he played for Nottingham Commercial versus Newark, and soon after he found himself playing amongst higher company in his first recorded three-day match, for the Nottingham Commercial Club, when 18 of them took on the All England Eleven at Trent Bridge on 4, 5 and 6 August. The match was for the benefit of the stylish old Nottinghamshire batsman, Joseph Guy: 'fit, sir, to play before Her Majesty in a drawing room', according to old Clarke, of whom more anon. Richard scored only six in the first innings and fared half as well in the second, but not one of the rest of the first twelve on his side did as well! Only five of the 18 reached double figures in their 36 innings. Butler Parr, Richard's future father-in-law, contributed two and four not out. For the All England Eleven, only Julius Caesar of Surrey achieved more than twenty, and the Commercial actually emerged victorious by 90 runs. Included in the England Eleven were Arthur 'Ducky' Diver, H.H.Stephenson, Cris Tinley, Guy himself, and John 'Foghorn' Jackson, all top-notch players. He must have attracted attention at Trent Bridge: certainly, John Johnson, a solicitor in Nottingham, was an early and enthusiastic supporter. Richard wrote that as a boy he learned the greater part of the game from two professional bowlers engaged with Nottingham Commercial Club: George Butler and Henry Hall. The club, founded in 1845, speedily became a power in Nottingham, and many of the leading players in the county were associated with it. George Butler, born in 1810, was a Mansfield man, who made 17 appearances for the county, starting in 1841: he appeared twice for the Players in 1843 and 1846. Harry

Hall was a left-arm bowler. Butler and Hall were employed in succession as head groundsman at Trent Bridge.

In June 1857, Richard put together scores of 13 and 17 when for Twenty-two of Loughborough, he faced the bowling of Clarke's England Eleven. He top scored in the second innings and took three wickets with his fast round-arm bowling. His most significant action, from a historical viewpoint, was that he held a catch. The victim was the ageing superstar, Alfred Mynn, who had made only two. He had been the champion all-rounder of the 1830s and 40s, a fearsome round-arm fast bowler and hard-hitting batsman. Perhaps the occasion of this match at Loughborough was the first meeting between these two giants of the game, Mynn with his best years far behind him and Richard on the threshold of his distinguished career.

In *Kings of Cricket*, Richard wrote: 'Mynn did not live to see me through a great part of my career, though he did live to see me attain many successes in the cricket field and paid me many kind compliments on my play.' He died at the end of October, 1861 following the rapid onset of diabetes. The tradition in Richard's family was that he made his first visits to Radcliffe in the company of Mynn who, when his cricket career was in decline, set up as a hop merchant. In the course of his travels, he met Butler Parr, who was the proprietor of a brewery in the village and was to become a member of the Notts county committee. The two became great friends and when visiting Radcliffe, Mynn took Richard with him. Butler Parr's origins were in Lincolnshire, but the village of Radcliffe was thronged with indigenous Parrs, among them the great Notts batsman, George Parr, who captained the county from 1856 to 1870. His family had farmed around the village for generations and occupied the Manor House. George was not a

Butler Parr, the senior member of the Parr clan in Radcliffe.

farmer and after his father, Samuel, died in 1857, he and his mother shared a much smaller house where Richard was their lodger for three or four years.

In the 1850s, Radcliffe was still a rural community, greatly under the influence of the local land owner, Earl Manvers, the vicar, and a few other local gentry. The village lay across the Trent about five miles to the east of Nottingham, and the populace were fiercely concerned to maintain their independence from the town and to oppose any action, such as the installation of main drainage, which might increase their rates.

When Richard was Parr's lodger, the two men passed the winters in shooting and fishing, often, as Richard wrote, in the company of Earl Stanhope, himself an able cricketer (and a distinguished historian); or in coursing with other friends. In one sense, this was the time of his life: his cricket was still developing in the summers of 1857 and 1858. He had no family ties and he widened his horizons as he lived the life of the country gentleman he longed to be. Whether George Parr was entirely a suitable mentor for him is somewhat doubtful. True, he was of good character and acceptable manners, and he was one of the most famous sportsmen in the kingdom, nicknamed the 'Lion of the North', but he was not a good example for a young man to follow. He deliberately never took up

George Parr,
recipient of Maori blessings and
Daft's mentor.

any other occupation than cricket-lucky man – don't we envy him – and later in life boasted that he had never had any intention of doing so. He added, with a beguiling lack of modesty, that if he had applied himself to developing his skills as a shot, he would have excelled his prowess as a cricketer!

Parr attributed his good fortune to a memorable incident on the tour which he led to Australia and New Zealand in the winter of 1863/64. After being on the losing end of an argument with the fast bowler, John Jackson, as to which of them should kiss the aged Queen of the Maoris, Parr, on taking the plunge, received a lucky charm of malachite from the monarch, who told him that as long as he possessed it, he would never have to do a hard day's work; 'and I never have,' he declared.

A month after the Loughborough match, Richard played at Derby when the local twenty-two opposed the All England Eleven, but this time there was a big development – he was playing for the Eleven. He scored only five in each innings and did no better for the Eleven against Twenty-two of Boston, but his last three matches brought much greater success. At Grantham, assigned to play for the local Twenty-two, his scores of 31 and 26 were the highest in each innings – the Twenty-two mustered only seven double-figure totals out of their 44 journeys to the crease! The season finished with five days of cricket at Irnham Park, under the generous hospitality of Captain W.H.Woodhouse. For Twenty-two of Irnham Park, he top-scored in each innings, compiling 35 and 29 against the United England Eleven attack which included John Wisden. He scored 8 and 26 for the Park against Old Harrovians. These last few innings were significant as they were made against strong amateur opposition.

In 1858, Richard hit his highest recorded score to date when he stroked his way to a total of 75 for the Notts Amateurs against Burton-on-Trent in June, and a week or so later he made his first-class debut at The Oval for Nottinghamshire against Surrey. This entry into the eleven was not quite as straightforward as this sentence suggests. The constitution of the Nottinghamshire side was the subject of a long letter from the Secretary of Surrey to *Bell's Life*. He had arranged to meet Lord Stamford (who had three of the Notts professionals, Bickley, Tinley and Brampton, contracted to play for him) to ask him to release them for the match, but Stamford would not be moved and ordered the three 'home'. In addition, George Parr was absent through illness.

In these circumstances, Richard was selected for the weakened Notts eleven to meet the best that could possibly have been thrown against them by Surrey. The home side ran up the considerable total of 200, but the last two batsmen fell to Richard. Going in at number three, Richard reached 13 before being bowled by an enormous break-back by Heathfield Stephenson. When Notts followed on, 86 in arrears, Alfred Diver (of Cambridgeshire) and Grundy gave them a second good start: the Notts captain varied the batting order and Richard, going in lower down, exhibited beautiful play and was undefeated on 44 as Notts reached 194, which left Surrey 109 for victory – a task they readily achieved early on the third morning.

Richard's performance led to his selection a week later by the Surrey authorities for the Gentlemen versus the Players, again at The Oval. Dismissed lbw for nought in the first innings, he atoned in the second when he and V.E.Walker scored freely in the course of a stand of 77 for the eighth wicket. Richard's contribution was 38 and as *Bell's Life* reported, in a statement which defies analysis, it was 'quite a cricket innings' as he defied an attack consisting of Jackson, Caffyn, Martingell, Wisden and Grundy.

In mid-July, he had a similar experience on his debut at Lord's, playing an unbeaten innings of 29 at his second attempt for North versus South after being run out for nine in the first. He did little in his remaining matches, so his final figures for the season in the eight matches which we now treat as 'first-class' were 210 runs at an average of 16.15, with a highest score of 44 not out. What a summer it had been! He had passed from his first county match to a successful appearance for the Gentlemen almost while you blinked, and gone on to appear in a number of representative sides. That first match for Notts was one of only two first-class games played by the county in the season. In truth, there was not enough county cricket to occupy the professionals or give them a living wage.

Chapter Three
The All England Eleven

'Many of our All-England XI matches were the pleasantest I ever took part in, for we were made much of by the supporters of the teams we played against, who generally did everything in their power to make us comfortable. ... The rough wickets were often the most disagreeable item in the matches; some of the batting was of a very second rate nature.' So wrote Daft in *Kings of Cricket*, adding that in a match in Cornwall, they got the local twenty-two out in 45 minutes!

William Clarke, a bricklayer and a publican by trade, first played for Nottingham in June, 1816, aged 17, and in the next thirty years never missed a major Nottingham fixture. However, he did not play in a representative match at Lord's until 1836 and did not become well-known nationally as a cricketer until the 1840s, his

The old Trent Bridge Inn, once William Clarke's domain, shortly before its demolition. Its replacement, opened in May 1885, is rising behind. Daft was licensee of the new building from 1896 to 1898.

formidable character and astute mind well attuned to money-making. In 1838, he opened the ground at Trent Bridge, having married in December 1837, as his second wife, Mrs Chapman, the landlady of the Trent Bridge Inn. Clarke would select and captain elevens of professional cricketers to tour the country, playing local sides composed of as many as eighteen or twenty-two to offset their lack of skill, and usually including a couple of professional bowlers, who would otherwise be members of the eleven, to provide stiff opposition to his batsmen. Assisted by the growth of the railway system, his professional eleven took good cricket all over Britain, and in due course spawned a number of off-shoots, rivals created by lesser entrepreneurs who were jealous of Clarke's success.

But membership of his eleven was the answer to a prayer for some professional cricketers: without him there would not have been enough cricket for them. County cricket was in its infancy: it was impossible for a professional to make a living out of county cricket until the sixties were well advanced. There were few matches, and plenty of amateurs often found places in county sides, to the exclusion of the pros.

In 1856 Clarke died, to be succeeded as captain and secretary of the All England Eleven, as well as captain of Nottinghamshire, by George Parr. In 1859, Richard became a regular member of the All England Eleven. The principal eight or nine full-time All England players were employed full time, first by William Clarke and later by George Parr: in 1851, the side played as many as 34 three-day matches, starting on 5 May and ending on 16 October. They were, wrote Richard, continually on the move, often travelling through the night; while the spread of the railways facilitated the growth of cricket, there were still plenty of small towns and villages beyond the end of the line. He remembered the drive over moorland in the dead of night, after a match at Redruth in Cornwall; there was enough light from the coach and frequent flashes of lightning to observe a deep ditch on each side of the track. When at last they arrived at their destination, the match itself was played on a very rough wicket. George Parr showed his greatness by scoring 101 runs in the match. Tom Hayward, who opened with Daft, was struck on the head by the ball which went straight up in the air and was caught by the wicket-keeper who had the coolness to appeal! This was only the first of the rather frail Hayward's disasters, as in the next match a throw-in by a fielder struck him on the heel.

One of the worst injuries was the one which Richard himself suffered at Salisbury: the batsman skied the ball straight up in the air and, as several fielders rushed in for the catch, Parr growled, 'Let Dicky have it.' Richard had it alright, but it struck the nail of his middle finger, tearing the greater part of it away from the flesh. More enjoyable, and perhaps safer venues were Grantham and Sleaford in Lincolnshire. The grounds would be crowded with the carriages of neighbouring landowners and farmers, 'for', Richard noted, 'farming in the country was then at its best.'

Richard included scores of some of the most significant (to him) games in *Kings of Cricket*. These included a match in June, 1861 against Twenty-two of Walsall, in which he scored 114 out of 305 – the Twenty-two mustered only 50 and 78. In 1868, he hit up 88 against Twenty-two of Bestwood at Bestwood Park in Nottinghamshire, in a match which the Eleven won easily by an innings. He bettered this performance against the same opposition a year later, achieving an undefeated 115 against an attack which included his old mentor, George Butler, who captured five wickets.

One of the liveliest members of the team was Julius Caesar from Godalming – the name continues down to this day in that part of Surrey. He was one of the smartest men Daft ever came across: his hitting, too, was clean and smart. He always travelled with a huge portmanteau, which he assured his colleagues was solid leather. Daft adds: 'It was a great deal too large for his needs, evidently, for whenever any amount of baggage was put on the top of it, it used to go down as flat as a pancake . . .' George Anderson was a terrific hitter, a fine looking man, six feet in height. He and Richard were both 'wretched sailors and used to suffer agonies whenever crossing the Irish Channel.'

Cris Tinley was unsurpassed at point; as an underarm bowler he was the best in England and also a very dangerous bat. George Tarrant was a grand fast bowler whose pace was tremendous and seemed even faster than it was on account of the long run he took. Daft had no doubt that the great amount of hard work Tarrant did in the cricket field shortened his life. Known as 'Tear 'em', he was five feet seven inches tall and weighed only a little over nine stone.

Daft wrote that John Wisden was 'for years one of the best all-round men in England, being a splendid fast bowler with a beautiful length, a grand little batsman and an excellent fellow withal.'

Daft's biggest set piece characterisations were reserved for George Parr, and Richard's own two greatest rivals with the bat in the 1860s, Tom Hayward senior and Robert Carpenter. Like Daft, they were all right-handers. Some contemporaries saw George Parr as a difficult man, tetchy and unpredictable, but Richard paints a more rounded picture. He was introduced into first-class cricket by old Clarke in 1844 when he was only 18 years old. Richard writes that Parr was the premier batsman of England. 'He was a good-looking man of medium height and of a very powerful build. His defence was a little clumsy as he always played very

Thomas Hayward (left) and Robert Carpenter were Daft's professional rivals and colleagues in the 1860s.
In first-class cricket, Hayward scored 4,789 runs at an average of 25.33, and Carpenter 5,220 at 24.39.

low down and was often much punished about the hands in consequence. His hitting all round was terrific.' Parr was famous, in particular, for his hitting to leg. Daft adds: 'All the team, especially we young ones, stood somewhat in awe of him, for George was always rather a queer-tempered man.'

If Richard's memories of his former colleagues were happy, others regarded them with hostility, not so much as individuals but as a class, because professional cricketers in their travelling elevens subverted the natural order of things. The opinions of many landed gentry were encapsulated by the well-known cricket historian, the Rev James Pycroft. 'Itinerary cricket', as he termed it, the falsely-called 'All England matches . . . a very serious nuisance . . . superseding those annual contests between rival counties which used to draw forth all the talent of the land.' It was immensely irritating to Pycroft and others that the Elevens deliberately encouraged their opponents to arrange fixtures on the same dates as county matches, particularly those involving Surrey.

In spite of Pycroft's tirades, Richard had no doubt about the value of the visits of the All England Eleven to country areas. 'Certainly', he wrote, 'one never sees such holiday-making and high jinks as we used to in the old All England days, especially at those matches played in small country towns. The All England match was the topic of conversation months before the event took place. Special committees were formed to get up entertainment in the evening, and when the great day arrived the excitement was often intense.'

Chapter Four
Professional

At the beginning of the season of 1859, Richard decided that he could no longer afford to play cricket at his own expense and turned professional. In future, he would be paid to play for George Parr's All England Eleven and for Nottinghamshire in the few matches which the county would expect to play each summer, as well as for the Players *against* the Gentlemen, North versus South, and other representative matches. The change, for Richard, would be immense: many years later, in 1886, the magazine *Cricket* commented that such a move by an amateur involved 'no small amount of courage' and that 'relations between amateurs and professionals, although pleasant, were well defined and strictly kept.'

Instead of wine and lunch in the pavilion, it meant pie and beer with the other professionals and the public in the tent: quite a scrimmage with the probability of offers of refreshment from the public, but there was so much more to face up to than that. English life was rigorously stratified. Many professional cricketers came from the higher reaches of the working classes, from the retail trades, or were craftsmen at the loom or frame or other light industrial work. Richard, with his inherited wealth, does not fit easily into this pattern. On the whole, the amateurs met their professional colleagues only on the field of play. They used separate changing facilities, almost invariably entered the arena through different gates and when playing away from home, lodged in separate accommodation, the players sometimes two to a bed in boarding houses, whilst the amateurs stayed at hotels. In the published scores, amateurs were designated 'Mr' or 'Esq': if the paid player was allowed his initials, they followed his surname. More often, no initials were given. Richard seemed in an ambiguous category all of his own. Many match scores simply called him 'Richard Daft'.

To some contemporaries, there was more to the status of 'a gentleman' than whether or not he was paid to play. Sir John Astley served with distinction in the Crimean War, finished his army service with the rank of colonel and inherited a baronetcy. He was perhaps proudest of his reputation forty years earlier as a runner over many varied distances when he wrote in 1894: 'In those days, mind you, an amateur meant a gentleman, whether he ran for money or honour or both – I used to combine the two . . .'

But not many would have cared to tell Sir John that he was not a gentleman. Mike Huggins, in *The Victorians and Sport*, confirms that the key distinction was between 'gentlemen' and the rest, with the object of limiting and stabilising what he describes as the democratic thrust of Victorian society. In horse racing, some events were restricted to 'gentleman riders' to avoid competition with the lower orders, and in the 1860s, when Richard was playing cricket as a professional, gentleman riders were the subject of specific definition, which included 'those persons generally received into society as gentlemen' or those belonging to a select list of London clubs, or officers on full pay, magistrates, peers, or even those persons successful in a ballot by the National Hunt Committee! Receipt of payment for participating was not one of the main criteria. The definition of a gentleman or an amateur depended on who you wanted to keep out.

In cricket, professionals were expected to know their place. The top professionals may have sighed for the days of Old Clarke, but the future of the game did not lie with the touring elevens. As W.F.Mandle wrote, their very success had encouraged the growth of local cricket and as it spread to the public schools as well, the middle classes and the aristocracy reasserted their control of the game and they revived county cricket. A county championship of sorts was adjudicated regularly by the cricket annuals and the press from 1864. The amateur/professional relationship continued in county cricket up to 1962. In a study published 25 years after that date appeared the following iconoclastic conclusion:

> All aspects of cricket were closely bound to a whole range of wider social tensions and tendencies. That it suffered less from open professional/amateur conflict (than did association and rugby football) was due to the ability of the amateur and the class he represented to disarm or subvert the clearly perceived threat of the professional and his class.

If this meant war – and there were skirmishes in the 1880s and 1890s when English professionals were affronted at the respect and remuneration paid to the Australians when they toured the United Kingdom designated as amateurs – Richard was only ever on the fringe of it towards the end of his career, when Nottingham professionals took umbrage over the terms the Australians enjoyed for playing against them at Trent Bridge in 1878. He was fortunate in playing for a county side which was almost always composed of fellow professionals and whose executives were mostly devoted to him.

By the end of June 1859, Richard had taken part in nine matches, eight of them for the All England Eleven, of which only two ranked as 'important'. Both were at Lord's in June, and he was totally unsuccessful. William Caffyn dismissed him twice for nought when the All England Eleven met their rivals, the United England Eleven. Later in the month Richard hardly did better, managing scores of only four and eight for North versus South.

In the Eleven's matches against odds, there was the usual ludicrously low scoring: after George Parr hit his century against Twenty-two of Cornwall at Redruth, the home side fell for scores of 22 and 30. A few days later, the Eleven did little better themselves at Wellington Park near Launceston, replying to their hosts' score of 58 with a total of 47, so Richard's contribution of 20 was something to be proud of.

Following his poor performance for the North at Lord's, Richard was not chosen for Players versus Gentlemen at The Oval, nor the All England Eleven versus United England Eleven at Lord's. He then made a return to form for Notts versus Surrey at The Oval, stroking his way to 52 out of 119 in the first innings before hitting his own wicket, and scoring 22 not out in the second. Everything in the match was put in the shade by the batting of George Parr, who compiled 130 for Notts. Richard batted at the top of his form against Twenty-two of Rutland on 28 July, when he placed the ball skilfully among the 22 fielders until he was caught with his total at 99.

It was at Ipswich in July this year that Richard first met Bob Thoms, the celebrated umpire, whom George Parr had asked to watch the 'young un' and give him his opinion. This Thoms did after the match over a cigar at the White Horse Hotel (it was at this rendezvous that Mr Pickwick got into the wrong bedroom). Thoms' opinion must have been favourable: Richard contributed 44 to his team's total of 103.

The lodestone by which a cricketer's reputation at the highest level was measured in the late 1850s and 1860s was performance in the matches between the All England Eleven and their rivals, the United England Eleven, which had been formed by John Wisden and some colleagues in 1852 when they broke away from William Clarke. Not surprisingly, these games had a real edge of competitiveness which made them more attractive. Richard's entry into the arena at Lord's in 1859 could not have been less successful, as we have seen, and he fared little better a year later when Caffyn again had him twice for nought and ten.

The first time Richard made any impact in the series was at Lord's in 1861 when his 48 in the second innings – the highest individual score in the match – contributed to an exciting finish. He did still better at Old Trafford in July, hitting up 66 before he was caught behind the wicket. In a third match between the two elevens at The Oval in August, he was twice dismissed by Griffith for nought and 25. However, after the season of 1862, Richard's appearances for the All England Eleven became fewer and fewer: indeed, his matches against odds reduced to one in 1863.

In 1864, he played in only eleven matches of note, six at Lord's or The Oval, three at Trent Bridge, one at Bradford, and the other at the Crystal Palace. In the first match of the season at Lord's, beginning on 16 May, which raised £102 5s 3d for the Cricketers' Fund, of which more later, his scores were 44 and 21, and in 1865, 25 and nought, when the Fund benefited to the extent of £268 9s 6d. Altogether that season, he played only three matches for the All England Eleven. His finest achievement in the series of matches came at Old Trafford in May, 1867. After J.C. Shaw had played the major part in dismissing the United for 208, Richard joined John Smith of Cambridge with the score at 31 for one. His partner reached 34 before being bowled, but only Richard displayed any fluency against an attack which included George Freeman, George Atkinson, George Howitt and Jemmy Grundy. The All England Eleven totalled 232 and he was left undefeated on 111, compiled without a chance. The authorities at Old Trafford, aware of the custom at The Oval where a successful batsman would be met on the pavilion steps by the Surrey Secretary and presented with a new bat, summoned, in the words of the reporter, 'the gentlemanly Daft to the pavilion for such a ceremony as a memento of his splendid cricket.' The United All England Eleven then collapsed, leaving All England to scramble home by four wickets – Daft was bowled by Freeman for four.

In the only match between the two elevens in 1868, played on the Savile Town Ground, Dewsbury, when almost all the participants were northern born, Richard contributed 36 and 14. In the next year he was in at the kill, when the Dewsbury Ground saw the last ever match between the two elevens.

George Parr finished with the highest average in the series:

	M	I	NO	R	HS	Ave	100	50
G. Parr	18	34	3	646	56*	20.83	-	3
R. Daft	14	27	1	529	111*	20.34	1	1
T. Hayward	14	27	0	469	67	17.37	-	1

A pivotal year for county cricket was 1864: county clubs were formed in Middlesex and Lancashire, over-arm bowling was legalised, and the name of W.G.Grace appears for the first time in published scores, though he was 15 going on 16, and these were not first-class appearances. An interesting feature was that Richard spent the first of two successive seasons coaching at Harrow, helping George Parr to teach the boys there in the company of Arthur Haygarth and the Hon Robert Grimston.

This early application to the game paid off in 1861 when, according to William Caffyn, 'the batting averages were larger than they had ever been before, Hayward, Daft and Carpenter all making over 1,300 runs for averages of more than 20' – remarkable figures for that time. Richard's opinion was: 'There was little difference between the three of us. Carpenter just beat Hayward and myself in eleven-a-side matches, but I was slightly the best against odds.' He goes on to refer to his score of 114 for the All England Eleven against Twenty-two of Walsall in mid-June: 'up to that time the largest score ever made against twenty-two.'

It was the end of May before Richard played in a match of any significance. For the All England Eleven against the United, as already noted, he excelled with 48 in the second innings. His next outing was at The Oval when the authorities had introduced a new invention – a house on rollers 'with figures for telegraphing on each side'. Richard hardly troubled the scorers, totalling only ten and three. His innings against Twenty-two of Walsall was one of the great features of the season as he opened the innings and was last out for 114, making his runs out of 305. In more distinguished company, Richard scored 65 at Lord's for Eleven Players of England against 16 Undergraduates of Oxford and Cambridge, and did it again there for the Players against the Gentlemen a week later.

Only once that season did he play in a county match at Trent Bridge. It was against Surrey, beginning on 25 July, when his scores of 22 and six added little to his season's large aggregate. Richard fared better in his next match, for England also against Surrey, which immediately followed at The Oval. His totals of 22 and 33 did not stop Surrey winning by 56 what was known as the 'Cripples' Match': seven of the Surrey side were playing in spite of injuries.

At Canterbury a fortnight later, in mid-August, for England against Fourteen of Kent, he accumulated 22 and 55, his second innings total being the only one over 40 in the match in which Kent were successful by 54 runs. Richard returned with Notts to Trent Bridge, where the opposition were Twenty-two of the County. The opposition included Thomas Daft and Charles Daft, who easily top-scored in the second innings with 24 before Richard caught him. Thomas was nearly 18 years older than Richard and a master joiner by occupation. He was never a major force in cricket, although he was at club level a useful bat and a good field at long-stop, who played for both Nottingham Commercial and Mapperley Park. Charles Daft was a good and steady batsman. His career for Nottinghamshire in first-class matches was short, extending only from 1862 to 1864. Probably his best innings was his 46 against Kent at Trent Bridge in 1864. He was better known as a hurdler who won many prizes.

It was not a very long journey from Trent Bridge to Gainsborough, also on the Trent, where the All England Eleven contested affairs with another twenty-two on 29, 30 and 31 August. After the disposal of the locals for 57, Daft opened the batting. Only Thomas Hayward gave him much support, yet some of the others must have stuck around as Richard batted on and on until the last wicket fell at 178, leaving him on 65 not out after six-and-a-half hours at the wicket! A collection realised around £175 in modern currency.

Richard finished the season with another long score, 58 against Twenty-two of Middlesbrough. This summer, he played 24 matches against odds and fourteen matches between teams of first-class status, but only two of them were for Notts, both against Surrey. In matches recorded in *Scores and Biographies* that year, he scored 1,248 runs.

Daft was tangentially involved with the English cricket tour to Australia, which was scheduled to take place during the winter of 1861/62, to the extent that like most of the senior English professionals, he refused to have anything to do with the adventure, although he claimed that he was told to name his price. Richard later told *Old Ebor* (A.W.Pullin): 'I declined to state a price. I could not see my way to go at the time.' So a team led by Heathfield Harman Stephenson left on *S.S.Great Britain* without him. Richard never made it to Australia.

Nottinghamshire's side of 1862, which won three of its four first-class matches. Standing (l to r): R.Daft, J.Grundy, G.Parr (captain), G.Anderson (umpire), Rev A. Bateman, J.Jackson, C.Brampton, J.Johnson (Honorary Secretary), G.Wootton and A.Clarke. On the ground: R.C.Tinley, C.F.Daft and S.Biddulph (wk).

Chapter Five
More at Home

Meanwhile, an increasing influence on Richard's life was Butler Parr, the brewer and a respected figure in Radcliffe-on-Trent. He had been a first-class cricketer who made his debut for Notts against Sussex in 1835, playing up to 1842, and then again for them from 1851 to 1854. When the Nottingham Commercial Club was formed, he scored heavily for them. Later, he was a member of the Notts Committee, from 1865 until his death in 1872.

In September 1862, Richard married Mary, aged 19, and the only daughter of Butler Parr, who had only one other living child, a son, also named Butler, who in 1862 was only three years old. There may have been other children but they had not survived. The existence of this little son and heir was to have unfortunate repercussions for Richard many years later, but as time went by the situation should have become clear to him. In 1856, Butler Parr senior had inherited a long-established brewery in Walker's Yard in the village, where Richard started work for him sometime before his marriage – he described himself as 'Agent' on his marriage certificate. In October

Daft's wife Mary, aged nineteen, painted at about the time of their marriage in 1862.

1863, when Mary registered the birth of their elder son, Richard Parr Daft, she described her husband as a 'Beer Agent', as did Richard himself when he registered the birth of Harry Butler Daft in 1866.

From the date of his marriage, Richard played less and less cricket for the All England Eleven. His travels diminished under the watchful eye of his father-in-law, as his participation in the brewery business came increasingly to the foreground. Soon, he came to have other interests of his own, for when his brother Thomas died, all too young at 49 in 1867, Richard as one of his executors is described as a cricket outfitter.

In 1862, his first first-class match of the season came at the end of May at Old Trafford, playing for North versus South. He then played for Notts against Cambridgeshire at Fenner's, when his 40 in the second innings helped his county to win by three wickets. The following week he contributed 36 to the All England Eleven's first-innings lead of 77 over the United All England Eleven, whose second-innings collapse enabled the All England Eleven to scrape home by four wickets, but it was then nearly six weeks before he again came to the fore when the North took on the South at Lord's, beginning on 21 July. His innings, described by *Scores and Biographies* as 'a splendid display of science' against the best bowling, continued until the North's score reached 233, to which Richard's contribution was 118. Ultimately, they gained victory by an innings and ten runs. William Caffyn wrote: 'One of the London papers declared that the Notts batsman had now immortalised himself! It certainly was a fine performance, as the wicket was a very bumpy one, even for Lord's. Daft batted for over four hours and never gave the ghost of a chance. He was at length out through an accident, Willsher hitting him on the hand and the ball dropping onto the wicket.' *Lillywhite's Guide* added: 'Daft was presented with a new bat, and if ever a new bat was deserved, it was by the 118 obtained at Lord's Ground by Richard Daft.'

Willsher was the central figure in an historic match at The Oval, which began on 25 August, 1862. At the end of the first day, England had reached 244 for three wickets, and on the second, with Carpenter scoring 94 and Hayward 117, they reached the dizzy heights of 503 by 5.30 pm. Shortly before 6 pm, Surrey sent in Mortlock and Thomas Humphrey to face the England attack. When Willsher bowled, the umpire John Lillywhite called 'no ball' and it went away for four: what happened next became historic. Lillywhite called each of the next four or five balls 'no ball'. A dramatic scene followed. Indignantly, Willsher threw the ball to the ground and left the field, soon followed after an interval by the rest of the England side, including Richard, and play ended for the day. Of the England team, eight members were northern professionals and some of them were deeply suspicious of The Oval authorities, believing that John Lillywhite had been put up to no-ball Willsher in the hope of saving Surrey from a humiliating defeat. The next day, the Surrey Committee directed John Lillywhite to stand down so that the match could continue without further interruption. Willsher, in turn, apologised for his hasty manner in leaving the ground. Richard's contribution to this drawn match was a duck.

Richard himself, ever discreet and tactful, wrote of this match: 'It cannot be denied that to the spectators who did not watch him most closely, he appeared to deliver above the shoulder. As a matter of fact, I believe that when the ball left his hand, it was exactly on a level with his shoulder. He came up to the wicket with a quick march kind of step, raised his hand high above his head, bringing it down, however, with a very quick jerky movement just as he delivered. That last movement of his seemed to put a spin and impetus on the ball that caused it to rise like lightning from the pitch. It seemed to reach one almost before it left his hand sometimes.' Richard accorded him the tribute of saying that he was the type of bowler a batsman, even one who was well set, was always glad to see taken out of the attack. Willsher had an equally high opinion of Richard's batting, and in connection with his back play to a good length ball, told Caffyn: 'When Richard plays that ball, I always feel as if he said, "If that's all you can do, Ned, you'd better put somebody else on at once!"'

The following year, MCC legalised over-arm bowling.

Richard was newly married and employed under the kindly but concerned eye of his father-in-law; but was marriage the only reason for his playing such a greatly reduced amount of cricket in 1863 and the following seasons? He was closely associated with George Parr, but in the years following 1859, their relationship was not necessarily beneficial for Richard. Parr was often at odds with his opponents from the South of England and Surrey, in particular. A catalyst was the match between the North and Surrey at the end of August, 1859. Parr took umbrage when the Surrey captain, F.P.Miller, refused to let him take on a substitute batsman in place of his injured wicket-keeper. Parr did not forgive or forget. In a year or two, he was declining to take part in any fixture played at The Oval. In 1863, Cambridgeshire withdrew from participation in matches with Surrey at The Oval because their three great professionals, Carpenter, Hayward and Tarrant, were staunch supporters of Parr.

Richard was one of the eight professionals from the North who played in the Willsher match, but the following year, 1863, he did not represent the Players at Lord's or at The Oval, nor did he turn out for England or the North when they played south of the Thames. On the other hand, he played only twice for the All England Eleven, once against the United at Lord's, when he scored only two and 11, in May, and once for the England Eleven against odds, and that not until mid-August. Haygarth in *Scores and Biographies* is quite clear that, owing to business, Richard's efforts were confined for some little while to the matches of his county and a few first-rate ones at Lord's.

That summer, he appeared in only nine matches of note, of which five were first-class, and of these four were for Notts – two each with Kent and Yorkshire. Richard began the season in good form, scoring 39 and 80 not out at Trent Bridge against Kent, who were set 282 to win; they were in the process of being overwhelmed at 41 for 6 when time ran out. Ten days later, Notts visited Great Horton Road, Bradford, for their initial first-class match with Yorkshire. The home side excelled, leading by 16 on the first innings, and then bowling Notts out for 88, to win by eight wickets. Richard top-scored with 27 in the first innings but was unable to stop the rot with 17 in the second.

The return at Trent Bridge a fortnight later came to a sensational close: Richard's totals were 20 and 25 in a low-scoring match in which Notts had to follow on 81 behind. They made a small recovery, seven batsmen reaching double figures, and left the strong Yorkshire side 101 to win. Ned Stephenson hit up 30 without difficulty, but a metamorphosis was imminent. A contemporary noted: 'One of the most exciting matches ever played in Nottingham. In the last innings, Yorkshire had only 30 runs to obtain, but owing to the splendid bowling of J.Grundy they were got out, leaving Notts the conquerors by six runs.'

The next match was against Kent at a novel venue, Swift's Park, Cranbrook. Richard made only ten but Kent did little better, scratching only 58 and 45, to lose by an innings, in the face of a wonderful performance by Jackson, who scored 100, took 12 wickets, and held three catches from the bowling of Grundy – the two bowled unchanged throughout the two Kent innings. Richard made a more prominent contribution to his last three-day match of the season for Notts versus Fourteen Free Foresters. This produced another thrilling finish when the county, set 212 to win, had struggled to 148 for nine. Biddulph, the last man, then joined George Wootton, and they slowly worked up the runs until the scores were level. Then Biddulph, though moving well forward, was given out leg before. In the first innings, Richard took out his bat for 26. His second effort of 56 was the only score over 30 for Notts, before the breathtaking last stand: other incidents in the last innings which contributed to the outcome were a call of 'one short' and, to balance, a no-ball was called but not recorded.

Richard earned an honourable mention in a long piece of versification sending another team on their way to the Antipodes, beginning:

> Twelve mighty cricketers of world-wide fame,
> Twelve Englishmen all highly known by name,
> Have lately left their native isle, to show
> What Britons in the cricket field can do.
>
> Jackson comes next; the ball his special care,
> His pace is awful:
> A Pilch, a Mynn, a Daft combined would take
> His balls to conquer and his bowling break.

Apart from business, Richard had an additional reason for staying at home. Ten days after the departure of the intrepid tourists, Mary Daft gave birth to her first child, a son, who was christened Richard Parr Daft, named after his father and grandfather.

Chapter Six

Comparisons

Fortunately for the narrative line, Richard spent more time on the cricket field in 1864, but it cannot be said that he was consistently successful. He did not play his first innings of note until the last week in June, when he stroked his way to 61 for the Players at The Oval. On the same ground, his scores were 56 and 29 for Notts versus Surrey, but bigger scoring was required from his side in the face of the Surrey score of 468. In the follow-on, after Richard was run out for 29, no-one did much and Surrey needed only four to win. A fortnight or so later, Notts met Kent on a new ground, at the Crystal Palace, where bumpy conditions made batting difficult. It was during Richard's display that Edgar Willsher said to his colleague in the Kent side, Captain McCanlis: 'This is the hardest wicket to bowl down in England.' McCanlis queried this: 'Have you forgotten Carpenter?' 'No!' came Willsher's riposte. Thanks to Richard's 78, Notts won by 74 runs.

A fortnight later, at Bradford, he played another match-winning innings, this time 80, which gave Notts victory over Yorkshire by seven wickets. Yorkshire's second innings was something of a curiosity: only seven wickets fell to the bowlers as B.W.Waud was run out, George Anderson retired hurt after being hit and George Atkinson, while bowling, had been taken out by a drive from Richard. He could not complete his over and had to be taken home. The boot was on the other foot at The Oval when Richard turned out for England against Surrey: Parr and Co had all declined their invitations and he may have wished he had done the same when, in the first innings, he received so severe a blow over the heart that he had to retire. On resuming, he was caught for only two. At the second attempt, he was run out for ten – an unhappy ending to his first-class cricket for the season.

Notts had had a mediocre summer, playing seven matches of which they won only three. Richard scored 334 runs in 13 innings at an average of 27.83 for the county: in all matches he hit 498 runs. His brother, Charles, scored 215 runs at an average of 15.35, bringing his total over three seasons to 392 runs at 14.00: 1864 was in fact the high point of his first-class career.

The Illustrated Sporting News had this to say about Richard in 1864:

> As a batsman, Daft, in my opinion ranks second to none in the world. Tom Hayward plays gracefully, but he is no more worthy to be compared to Daft in gracefulness than I'm fit to be Chancellor of the Exchequer; Bob Carpenter hits splendidly to the off and keeps down the balls well, but Richard Daft beats him hollow. Some exception has, I am aware, been taken to the fact that many off balls that other players would punish, Daft contents himself with playing back to the bowler. . . . Some judges say that since he ceased to play with the All England Eleven there has been a falling off in his batting, and I am inclined to think there is some truth in this opinion. As a fielder, he stands very high. He usually stands 'long-leg' and 'middle wicket off', and the sharpness and precision with which he returns the ball to the wicket are absolutely astonishing.

George Parr used to say that as a batsman, Hayward was much more showy than Carpenter but altogether inferior to him. Of their playing contemporaries, Edward Rutter, who bowled slow left arm for Middlesex and Southgate, considered that Richard was nearly as good as Hayward. Alfred Lubbock, a brilliant bat for Eton, Kent and the Gentlemen, liked the batting of Daft and Hayward the best. W.G.Grace, who was so soon to dwarf them all, said of Richard:

> He was the most finished and graceful batsman in England for a great many years. From 1859 until 1876 he was the most scientific batsman among the professionals, delighting everyone by his upright, manly style of defence and exceptional wrist power. He was a fine field at long-leg, and that, too, at a time of rough kicking grounds. He made an excellent captain and led the Players and Nottinghamshire to many a victory.

Richard and Robert Carpenter died within a year of one another, and in their obituaries in *Wisden's Cricketers' Almanack*, almost certainly written by the editor Sydney Pardon, the writer expressed a considered view:

> [Richard Daft] came before the public at about the same time as Robert Carpenter and the late Thomas Hayward, and for three or four seasons it was a disputed point as to which of the three

was the finest bat in England. ... Whether Daft was as good or better than Hayward or Carpenter is purely a matter of opinion, but there can be no question that in their day all three were very great indeed. It is a fair criticism to say that, while Daft and Hayward were far ahead of Carpenter in point of style, Carpenter's was perhaps the hardest wicket to get.

A year later, *Wisden* described Carpenter as one of the really great batsmen of his time. This time, Richard did not figure in any comparisons.

But the performances of Richard and his contemporaries were serving only as the overture to an altogether bigger composition. By his novel variety of strokeplay, by his unyielding keenness at the crease and in the field, by his ability to play the game day in and day out from April to October, and to pile up the runs against all-comers and to take more than his share of wickets, W.G.Grace was to become the most vibrant force in cricket and he remained as such through several generations of cricketers until the 1890s. In the public mind, he eclipsed all that had gone before. He was not held back by the fact that, as yet, there was no Gloucestershire county side to play for.

Chapter Seven
County Cricket

'If one county is better than any other, that county is Nottingham', said *John Lillywhite's Cricketers' Companion* reviewing 1865. The county was strengthened by the arrival of Jemmy Shaw, a fast left-arm bowler of rare skill, in spite of a remarkable and disconcerting squint. This did not affect his skill with the ball, but may have been responsible for his almost total ineffectiveness as a batsman, who reached double figures only once in eleven seasons with the county. Aided by other new acquisitions, Alfred Shaw and William Oscroft, Notts completed a successful, if still restricted, programme of seven fixtures, beating Sussex and Yorkshire twice, Surrey once and Cambridgeshire, too, in their only fixture, while they lost to Surrey in the return by one wicket.

In 1865, Richard's season began with failure against sixteen Notts Colts at Trent Bridge and against Twenty-two of Retford for the All England Eleven, but neither his failures nor appearances against odds were typical of this season: nor was the All England Eleven a typical All England team. It now consisted entirely of players from the North: Willsher and others had helped to form the rival United South of England Eleven. Richard batted well for the county in their first match against Sussex at Trent Bridge, accumulating 67 and adding 122 with George Parr for the fourth wicket, a county record. Sussex scored 84 and 38 in the face of devastating bowling by Grundy. At Lord's, Richard fared adequately for the All England Eleven against the United, scoring 25 in his first innings. This was the occasion when Grundy bowled 84 balls to George Parr and Richard without their scoring a run, except two from an overthrow. The following week, Richard played a brilliant innings of 78 for North versus South.

On the evening of the second day of that game, the Cricketers' Fund Friendly Society held its Annual General Meeting at Lord's. Willsher, Tinley, Carpenter, Grundy, Tarrant, Daft, H.H.Stephenson and John Wisden were all present. Tom Box announced his resignation as Chairman. Subsequently, Richard was elected as a member of the Committee of Management, and was then asked to take the chair and presided over a great deal of business. Wisden was re-elected Treasurer. It was a compliment to Richard that he was elected to the post at the age of only 29. He also chaired the Society's Annual General Meeting on 3 July, 1871, but whether he held office continually from 1865 onwards it is not possible to say. Only by the middle of the century was there a sufficient number of active professionals to make such an organisation feasible.

A fortnight later at Trent Bridge, Richard was undefeated for a score of 52 in Notts' second innings against Surrey. The match terminated with a fine stand between Richard and Tom Bignall, and victory for Notts by eight wickets. In July, at Bradford, his innings of 66 was the only 50 in the game and contributed, along with the bowling of Jackson, Jemmy Shaw and Tinley, to victory over Yorkshire by an innings and 30 runs. This was a controversial fixture as the home side had been raised by a committee in Bradford rather than by the one in Sheffield, where Yorkshire cricket's power base then lay. Notts were successful by a wide margin, but the event passed off amicably enough. In the next match, in which Surrey were the hosts, George Parr still refused to play at The Oval, so the match may have started in an atmosphere of ill-will: it proved a closely contested game. Surrey, who batted second, had a first-innings lead of 13 and were ultimately set 195 to win. In spite of a grand innings by H.H.Stephenson, who opened the innings and was still batting, with 75 runs to his credit, 14 were still required when the last man, Tom Sewell, went in. He proceeded to hit off the runs required all by himself, but a decision of the umpire in his favour gave the Notts players so much offence – he was run out by a yard-and-a-half, declared William Oscroft – that the Notts players and committee declared that they would not renew the fixture.

The year 1866 began with a touch of farce. In January, the press reported George Parr's continuing hostility to the Surrey club and his refusal to allow any player 'of whom he has control' to play at The Oval. It was the opinion of F.S.Ashley-Cooper that this declaration concerned no-one but Parr himself. A month later, Richard appeared in pantomime! The Nottingham Theatre staged *Jack and the Beanstalk*, and the Notts team appeared on stage in cricket dress, while Miss Clara Denvil, in the character of Jack, delivered a rhyming address about each in turn:

This quarrel, call'd by some, 'The Cricket Schism' –
Distasteful term! in fact, a barbarism!
But some there be who other feelings stir up,
And one of those, I fear, is Mr.Burrup[1]
Whose latest insult to our county's team
Is "That a chicken-hearted lot they seem."

[Scene drawn and Notts Eleven 'discovered']

But here they are, and, for a cowardly crew,
They don't so badly look; "George, how d'ye do ?"
Now let us, if we can, find out who may be
In the Notts team, a "chicken-hearted" baby.
How you would derisively have laughed
Had I term'd funky Oscroft here, or Daft. . . .

In 1866, Notts played only six matches; to these Richard added only one other first-class game – for the All England Eleven against the United at Lord's in May, though he did play six times against odds which was more than for some years past. When Harry Butler Daft was born on 5 April, the father gave his occupation to the Registrar not as a cricketer but as a brewery agent, a clear indication as to where his energies were principally directed at this time.

The All England match at Lord's was played for the benefit of the Cricketers' Fund and took £267 9s 0d at the gate, which must have pleased Daft as Chairman, but in this match he suffered the most painful injury of his whole career. A debutant in the match was George Howitt: his bowling technique consisted of erratic deliveries, a hideously fast break-back from the off, and bumpers, and at Lord's he felled Richard with a blow on the chin. Nearly fifty years later, a spectator recalled: 'I remember seeing Daft in a match at Lord's receive a horrible crack from a bumping ball – a blow so severe that he became rigid with the pain. Old Tom Lockyer, who was behind the stumps, had him in hand almost as he fell, and administered vigorous massage which brought Daft round to face the bowler. . . . The second ball delivered set our hero free to walk unsteadily to the pavilion.'

It was six weeks before Richard made runs in a big match when he hit 52 for Notts against Cambridgeshire. In two rare appearances

---

1   William Burrup was the Surrey secretary from 1852 to 1872.

for the United he made 30 and 18 at Sutton-in-Ashfield, and then nine versus Dewsbury in the last week in July, but he did not then play an innings of note for another fortnight until Notts travelled South to meet Middlesex at Islington. Though he failed in the first innings, when Notts led Middlesex by two runs, he played a splendid innings of 94 when they went in again.

When the Notts County Cricket Club held their general meeting in December, John Johnson resigned as secretary and afterwards entertained a party consisting of Notts supporters and the county eleven to a lavish dinner. George Parr, on behalf of the county side, presented Johnson with a splendid silver goblet on a salver, inscribed by Parr himself, Richard and the other members of the team.

Wisden's Cricketers' Almanack next year commented on the great increase in the number of matches played during the 1866 season, but Richard's participation was limited to seven appearances, six of them for Notts, and his form suffered for lack of match play.

In Notts matches he scored 229 runs at 22.90 and in all first-class games he reached 255 at 21.25. By contrast, at this time, his bowling colleagues at Notts, some of them MCC professionals, often played for the Club and other sides, and thus kept their skills well-honed throughout the season.

Playing even less frequently the next season, he benefited from a number of not-out innings to increase his average to 53.85, but he played only six first-class matches, of which five were for Notts. The reason is easy to see. In addition to his work at the brewery and his family responsibilities, he had set up on his own in Nottingham as a cricket outfitter. His life was further complicated by the death of his brother Thomas in February, 1867 at the comparatively early age of 49. As executor, with his cousin William Wood, Richard proved the will on 9 July and it is notable that before that date, he appeared only three times in first-class cricket. In one of these he scored his celebrated 111 not out against the United, while he was undefeated at Islington for scores of 72 and 18 against Middlesex in June.

These games formed Notts' full programme for the season, with the exception of a match against the North at Trent Bridge, beginning on 26 August. While Richard and the other Northern professionals were disporting themselves in this match, another was being played at The Oval between a combined team of Surrey and Sussex and a side labelled England, for the benefit of Tom Lockyer, who netted over £330. The England team was composed almost entirely of players from the South. At Trent Bridge, the two sides consisted of professionals, with one exception. The playing of these two matches on the same day exemplifies the continuing great rift between the North and the South, as represented by the authorities at The Oval. As far as Lord's was concerned, no Yorkshire or Cambridgeshire players were available to participate in matches there, while the Cambridge men refused to turn out at Bramall Lane, Sheffield, because, they claimed, it was on that ground that the Yorkshire Committee had previously arranged a match with Surrey! We get hardly any idea of what this was all about, but this season MCC decided that they had had enough of these recalcitrant pros and passed a resolution to set up a trust to support professionals who conducted themselves to the entire satisfaction of the Committee.

The match for the benefit of the Cricketers' Fund was played, not at Lord's, but at Old Trafford, and all the players came from the North.

The season of 1868 was tremendously hot. It saw the visit to this country of the Australian Aboriginals - but Nottinghamshire did not play them, though the Nottingham Commercial Club did. The

The diversely-clad Nottingham Commercial side, which played the Australian Aboriginal team at Trent Bridge in 1868, included Richard Daft's older brother. Standing (l to r): A.Fewkes (wk), C.F.Daft, A.Poyser (umpire), T.Wright, G.M.Royle, G.Rossall, W.Clements, R.Tolley. On the ground: J.West, S.Brittle, W.T.Palmer, J.Billyeald.

county played only six first-class matches, but their form was good enough for the press to adjudge them champions. Their opportunities to shine were limited – compared with those, for example, of Surrey, whose programme extended to 16 matches. Richard scored 285 runs, playing in all the games. He showed what fine form he might have produced in a full season's batting on the hard pitches: his first effort at Trent Bridge was a sparkling 94 against Lancashire at the end of May, leading to a handsome victory for Notts by an innings and 74 runs, as Lancashire crashed for 74 and 148.

In that fading centrepiece between the All England Eleven and their United opponents at Dewsbury, his 36 in the first innings was exceeded only by the unbeaten 40 of the United keeper, Tom Plumb. The game, over in two days, was for the benefit of Carpenter and Hayward and raised £335 14s 1d at the gate. Richard hit 61 for the All England side against Mr. Thomas Walker's Eighteen and went on from Eastwood Hall, near Nottingham, to Trent Bridge to fall for nought and 21 against Eighteen of the Nottingham Commercial Club. He hit fifties against Surrey at The Oval – a sign of reconciliation, perhaps – and Yorkshire at Savile Town, Dewsbury. In August, he amassed another big score against odds - Twenty-two of Bestwood Park fielded out his 88 runs. Altogether that summer, he again played as few as seven matches in first-class cricket, scoring 335 runs in 13 innings at an average of 25.76.

In 1869, now aged 33, he showed such good form that it is a source almost of grief that he did not play so very much more often than he did. In eleven innings for Notts, he scored 471 runs, averaging 67.28. It is noteworthy that he appeared again at both Lord's and The Oval and did so with remarkable effectiveness. At Lord's, his 103 not out in Nottinghamshire's second innings against MCC took him five hours on a typically difficult wicket and earned the praise of the *Wisden* commentator: 'For cool, scientific, cautious and successful defence, this innings of Daft's was a marvel; "slow" it certainly was, but it was "sure."' How hard run-getting was at Lord's before the middle 1870s is demonstrated by the fact that this match was the only one of the season there to extend to the third day. Notts had a lead of 17 on the first innings, in which W.G. scored 48 for MCC. When Notts batted again on the second day, Richard's innings commenced at 12.25 pm with the total 33 for three. While he was rocklike and immovable at one end, Shaw and

Wyld attacked at the other. With Wyld he added 78 for the fourth wicket and with Shaw, 98 for the fifth. The county's score increased by 262 before the innings ended at 6.50 pm when he remained undefeated. If Tuesday had been Richard's day, Wednesday belonged to W.G., who wagered that he would better Daft's fine effort and, attacking from the word go and giving several chances, scored 75 out of the MCC total of 119 for four. Eventually, with the score at 186, he was bowled off his pads, sixth out for 121 and so won his bet. This effort was unavailing as MCC subsided to defeat by 102 runs. This was the first time that Richard and W.G. had met on the cricket field and there was, from the first, a competitive edge when they did so.

The other innings of Richard's in 1869 which set enthusiasts talking was his 93 not out against Surrey at The Oval at the end of July. The home side were out for 206 on the first day when Notts were well placed at 68 for one. Next day, Richard went to join J.G.Beevor with the score of 96 for 3 at 12.50 pm. The partnership took the score to 173. Price hit hard and well while adding 95 for the sixth wicket, and after five hours' carefully judged batting, Richard was left undefeated on 93 when the innings ended for 356 – a lead of 150. His innings included 57 singles and only two fours. Jupp and Humphrey made a good response for Surrey with a stand of 107. Jupp seemed immovable: frustration set in as a drawn game seemed in prospect. Richard wrote: 'But at last I went on myself with my lobs and took five wickets for very few runs, Biddulph stumping four off me.' The last five wickets fell for ten runs. Harry Jupp was left high and dry with 102 not out. In earlier years, Gerald Brodribb tells us, Richard had occasionally bowled medium-fast round arm. For a few years from 1869 he took, under his own captaincy, a larger share in the attack but the fancy did not last. Notts were left with under 60 to get and struggled to achieve them for the loss of four wickets with 15 minutes to spare.

Notts were successful in four other county matches and lost only one, Yorkshire winning by five runs at Sheffield in spite of Richard's contributions of 50 and 31 not out. He played a typical innings, accumulating 56 in the other match with Surrey at Trent Bridge, though *Lillywhite's Companion* ('Green Lilly') described the Notts' fielding in the visiting side's first innings as simply disgraceful, rendering Surrey's innings a complete travesty of county cricket. Against Twenty-two of Bestwood Park at the beginning of August, he amassed the fine score of 115 not out. He hit a third century – 101 against Bulwell – during this season.

A notable absentee from cricket this year was George Parr who played only once for Notts. Two years later, in 1871, Richard formally took over the captaincy; by then he had already served a dozen years in the county side and had accumulated experience of leadership in the frequent absences of George Parr.

Richard Daft in the 1860s,
a leading batsman of the time.

Chapter Eight
Nottinghamshire Captain

Familiar figures leaving the county eleven included Alfred Clarke (1863), Jackson (1866), Grundy (who last played in 1867), Brampton in the same year, and Cris Tinley (1869). The year 1870 saw the last of George Howitt, who left Notts for Middlesex, and, in tragic circumstances, the promising young batsman, George Summers. Richard himself, Jemmy Shaw, Bignall, Oscroft, Wyld and Alfred Shaw straddled the period, though Alf's time as the emperor of bowlers was yet to come. The seventies saw a great enrichment of the eleven as John Selby, Fred Morley, Billy Barnes, Arthur Shrewsbury, William Scotton, Wilfred Flowers and Mordecai Sherwin forced their way into the team. All went on to represent England in the Test Matches, which became an increasingly important feature of cricket after 1876/77. Richard, as captain, was in the right place at the right time: this was to become one of the strongest county teams in history. How tested he was in leading this side of outstanding cricketers and characters we shall find out.

The Notts fixture list in 1870 was still limited to seven matches – compared with Surrey's 18. Richard appeared in the first six games before his play was brought to a premature end by an injury in August. For Notts, his figures were 495 runs at 61.87, far ahead of the county's second-highest scorer William Oscroft, with 194 runs at 17.63. In all first-class cricket Richard scored 565 runs at 51.36, an average exceeded in the season only by W.G. himself.

Richard had first led Notts in 1862 when Parr was absent and continued as a stand-in captain until 1870, taking over entirely in 1871 - Parr had played only four matches in 1870. The captain celebrated his 'appointment' by presenting the team with new caps, which were black with cherry-coloured ribbon piping down each seam. It seems that the leadership simply 'devolved' to Daft as Parr's 'right-hand man', without as far as is known, any formal decision being made by the County Club's executive.

The first county side met by Notts was Surrey at The Oval – a sure sign of reconciliation between North and South – beginning on 9 June. This was the first county match at The Oval in 1870, and a large crowd was present each day. In the first innings, Richard hit 55 before he hit his own wicket; Notts on 161 had a lead of 15. In the second innings, Richard top-scored with 80. According to *Wisden*, he played true bowling 'with an ease and science which was a pleasure to watch.' The Notts innings reached 325, leaving Surrey 341 to win. Jupp, yet again, held the line for Surrey in a long stand with Stephenson; they really collared the bowling in adding 99. Two of Stephenson's scoring shots (fives) resulted from overthrows. The tail took some dislodging, and it was 6.35 pm before the last wicket fell at 232, leaving Notts winners by 108 runs.

The next Notts fixture was also in London, at Lord's against MCC, two days after the finish of The Oval game. The match, which was full of incident, produced a major breach of the Laws of Cricket and was the scene of a dreadful accident. V.E.Walker played for MCC when Notts batted first until he suffered a hand injury and had to retire. When MCC's turn to bat came, H.A.Richardson went in instead of Walker – in each innings. There was to come a time, thirty years later, when such a breach of the law would result in sharp criticism from the MCC Committee and loss of first-class status of the fixture, but in fact at this period the allowing of substitute to bat was not particularly uncommon.

In his massive statistical survey of W.G's career, J.R.Webber suggests that Richard was pressurised into agreement to the substitution. Richardson, in turn, failed to turn out on the third day and another substitute, Price, fielded in his stead! The match, as it had been in 1869, was the only first-class fixture played at Lord's that season to last into the third day, and as in the previous year, both Daft and W.G. reached three figures. *Wisden's* report says that Richard never scored so rapidly as he did in making his 117. Only Summers, with 41, gave him any real help: their addition of 119 was the county's highest third-wicket partnership to date. Richard was eventually bowled, leaving at 238 for eight.

In a demonstration of approval, rare to Lord's, Daft was called up to the pavilion and presented with a prize bat. W.G. and I.D.Walker had taken MCC's score to 67 by the end of the first day's play, and next morning they added 35 at a run a minute and went on to 127 before Walker was dismissed. W.G. continued in great form, but the last nine wickets fell for 56. W.G. was left high and dry – his score equalling Richard's. MCC failed by four runs to avoid the compulsory follow-on. Straightaway, Jemmy Shaw bowled W.G. for a duck, but MCC left the county 157 to win. George Summers went in on the fall of the first wicket at 23. As Richard recalled to *Old Ebor* nearly thirty years later: 'Platts' deliveries got up as high as the batsman's head, and when he bowled to Summers, the first ball shot up extra quick and hit poor Summers on the left cheekbone. Reeling like a tee-to-tum [a small spinning top marked with letters for playing a game of chance], he collapsed to the ground unconscious. W.G., who was then a 21-year-old medical student, felt his pulse and said 'he is not dead', and Summers was carried to the Lord's Hotel.'

A number of contemporary attitudes are revealed by the descriptions of the incident by various participants. C.E.Green, the wealthy benefactor of Essex county cricket, commented: 'I could see by the way he clenched his hands that he had received some serious injury. Richard Daft had to come in next and I shall never forget seeing him walk in with a towel or two tied over his cap to cover his head. It showed what he thought of the dangers of the wicket,' and as Professor Derek West added, the proclivities of the bowler. Lord Harris, the captain of Kent, and for sixty years a moving force in the game, wrote: 'The next man to come in to bat was Richard Daft, who was always very dapper and rather full of self-importance. I shall never forget his coming out of the pavilion with two large towels bound round his head.'

The truth is that Daft wore one large towel round his head, covered with a scarf tied under his chin. He very nearly fell victim to Platts' next ball which pitched about halfway, shot up and went clean over his head. This was a clear indication that none of the gentlemen on the MCC side had warned Platts to hold his fire. Richard later commented: 'Platts' next ball would have hit me in about the same place had I not thrown my head back – as it was it passed me and went right away to the long stop.' C.I.Thornton, the great hitter, confirms Richard's arrival at the wicket in his safety covering and his avoidance of the first ball, and adds: 'Daft did let Platts have it and no mistake . . .' Platts, described by David Frith as a small but tremendously fast bowler from Derbyshire, who could swing the ball pronouncedly, is said to have lessened his pace after this distressing match.

As for poor Summers, after a rest he insisted on returning home to Nottingham where, on 19 June, four days after the accident, he died two days short of his 26th birthday. The MCC Committee provided his tombstone. Some declared that the money would have been better spent on their pitch. The Notts innings went on and Richard, in spite of the awful incident, continued his good batting before his dismissal, fifth out at 103. Biddulph, at last, made the winning hit, leaving Notts winners by a notional two wickets. Even then controversy was not at an end when it was discovered that, because of a mistake by the scorers, the total had already reached 158 at the fall of the eighth wicket and the victory was already Nottinghamshire's!

Another match with Yorkshire, at Trent Bridge, brought frustration to the home side. Notts were set 175 for victory: seven were needed as the last man, Jemmy Shaw, joined Howitt. The great Yorkshire fast bowler, George Freeman, remembered: 'I couldn't bowl at the finish as I'd hurt my arm. When things were getting desperate, Richard Daft protested against Emmett changing ends a third time (which the law did not then permit) and his appeal was upheld by the umpires. I beckoned to Rowbotham, Yorkshire captain, to put Lockwood on; he did so and Ephraim got the last two wickets for five runs and we won . . . ' In the return at Sheffield, Richard scored 45 not out and 46, the highest scores in the match: Yorkshire were left 142 to win, but were 35 short, with four wickets to fall, at the close of play.

More satisfactory to Notts was the match against Kent at Trent Bridge at the end of July, 1870. Richard easily top-scored with 49 in the county's innings of 201; he had outrun Kent who mustered only 41 and 73. The return with Kent at the Crystal Palace was described by *Wisden* as 'a brief and one-sided affair.' It was briefer still for Richard: he shared a stand of 88 with Robert Butler, George Parr's nephew, was well set and playing easily when, at 41 as he started for a run, one of the tendons of his left leg gave way. 'I heard it snap like a pistol shot,' said Richard, who hopped to the other end to make the run. He was then carried to the tent, given temporary repairs, and went home the following day to play no more that summer. As far as the match was concerned, Notts' score of 167 sufficed for an innings victory as Kent again crumbled. Richard went to recuperate at Mablethorpe. He hobbled into the sea on crutches every morning so that he should not miss the pleasure and benefit to be derived from sea bathing.

Chapter Nine
The Graces and the Counties

'From 1871 to the end of my connection with first-class cricket, county matches were more interesting than any others.' So wrote Richard in *Kings of Cricket*. Spice was added by the addition, in 1871, of the newly-formed county of the Graces.

Notts' only defeat in 1871 was at Sheffield where Yorkshire were victorious by 140 runs, and were generally acknowledged as the county champions. This was the year of W.G.'s first appearance in Nottingham and the event was eagerly anticipated. Richard himself was in splendid form, scoring in nine innings for the county 390 runs at an average of 65.00. His summer began as usual on Easter Monday when he scored 21 for the county Eleven against Twenty-two Colts, in front of a windswept crowd of 4,000. In his initial first-class foray for North versus South at Lord's, he did not get beyond the teens in either innings. He then had a month away from the game before turning out in Notts' first county fixture against Yorkshire at Trent Bridge: their great character and left-arm opening bowler, Tom Emmett, bowled him for nought, but his undefeated 50 in the second innings brought success to Nottinghamshire.

Back in London for what was already the height of the season, he failed to score for the Players at Lord's, falling to left-armer David Buchanan. At The Oval, he fell again to Buchanan for 11 in the return played back to back against the Gentlemen, but made reparation with an undefeated innings in the follow-on, when the Players attempted unsuccessfully to save the match. On the third day, in front of a crowd numbering 9,000, Richard, with Alfred Shaw, 38, put on 91 to carry the score to 260, which was 143 ahead, and the match was moving towards a draw. Then Buchanan dismissed Shaw and the last two men in the space of seven balls without addition to the score. Richard was left on 68 not out. The Gentlemen scored 145 in an hour and three-quarters to win the match for the loss of five wickets. He again reached 68, once more undefeated, later in July at Trent Bridge. As Notts totalled only

168, this was a fine effort by Richard – all the finer when you consider that Surrey's two innings, 48 and 63, amounted to only 111.

Notts' next opponents were the almost new Gloucestershire side, so recently but perfectly formed that almost every match set up some sort of record. This was the first time the two teams had played each other and was the first county match played on the Clifton College ground. The home side had the better of the play, heading Notts by 51 on the first innings and setting them 247 in 2 hours 25 minutes to win. Richard, who had contributed 34 to Notts' first-innings total, came in the second time at 17 for two. Following the dismissal of Wyld at 53, he and Selby made a stand which dispersed any notion of defeat: Richard was unbeaten on 51.

There was not much stopping Notts that summer. They defeated Surrey at The Oval by ten wickets; Richard gave a masterly exhibition in achieving his highest total of the season, 92. This included a record sixth-wicket partnership of 132 with Alfred Shaw, the highest for the county at the time. Ten days later Richard was home again at Trent Bridge. This match saw Gloucestershire, of course, achieving another first – their appearance at Nottingham. The presence of W.G. attracted large crowds – 25,000 visitors over the three days in delightful weather. E.M.Grace related that before the start of the game, bets of 20-1 were laid against W.G. getting a century in either innings. But everyone had to wait and see as Richard won the toss and the home side went to the crease, greatly to the disappointment of the crowd, and batted on until the second morning. Richard himself, going in at 120 for two, first put on 61 with Bignall, whose 96 was one of the finest innings of his career, and in company with the young amateur, Tolley, added a further 92. He was eventually out for 84 to a marvellous catch low down by W.G. at mid-off. There was, indeed, no keeping that hero down. At the start of the match, he kept wicket in the absence of the regular stumper, R.E.Bush. To emphasise his enormous energy, W.G. fielded at long leg both ends – except when he was bowling. He then played a fine innings of 79, but Gloucestershire had to follow on. There followed an exchange between Richard and the great man:

> *Richard*: You ought to have made a hundred – it's never been done in a first-class match on this ground.

W.G.: Why didn't you tell me earlier, and I'd have done it? Never mind, I'll do it next innings.

And he did, batting superbly for 116, and in doing so completing his thousand runs in the month of August, when there were still eight days to go. It was the first time the feat had been achieved in any month. W.G. gave no chance, but Notts were victors by ten wickets in this memorable contest.

Richard and W.G. met again at the Brunswick Ground, Hove, in the last first-class game played at the 'ground by the sea', for the benefit of John Lillywhite. There were 13,000 people present when W.G. opened for the Gentlemen, but Jemmy Shaw dismissed him first ball with a delivery which broke back sharply. When he walked in to bat the second time, he would have gone early again if Richard had held on to the simplest of chances: but the sun was in his eyes. Now the crowd could revel in the best of Grace; in four hours of splendid batting, he hit 31 fours and with Fred Grace put on 241 in 150 minutes. W.G. also captured seven wickets.

At the end of the season, the averages showed W.G. first and Daft, best of the rest, some way behind:

	M	I	NO	R	HS	Ave	100	50
1 W.G.Grace	25	39	4	2739	268	78.25	10	9
2 R.Daft	12	19	4	565	92	37.66	-	6

At this stage, their career figures read:

		M	I	NO	R	HS	Ave	100
W.G.Grace	1865-71	85	139	16	7379	268	59.99	26
R.Daft	1858-71	125	220	29	5422	118	28.38	4

These figures reveal a contradiction between W.G., apparently an amateur, cricketing on every available occasion, and so producing statistics the like of which had never been known before, and the limited input of Daft, a professional for whom, with his county's limited fixture list and so many other irons in the fire, the game seemed to be not much more than a hobby. Yet his standing in the game and in his own locality remained high:

Great is the hand-clapping, expressive of 'see the conquering hero comes' at Trent Bridge, when Daft, well aware of his importance, walks up to the wicket. He takes a good position in Nottingham and the name of Richard Daft, Esq figures in the subscription lists of the neighbourhood. He has great weight with the County Committee [and] possesses what is as valuable to the cricketer as the angler – pith and brains, pluck and judgement.

In Radcliffe-on-Trent, Richard was a prestigious inhabitant, his upright figure conspicuous as he drove towards Nottingham or walked to the station on his way to a day at the races, or set off for one of his other favourite spectator sports, a prize fight in a sequestered spot away from the eyes of the authorities. The arrival of the railway in 1850 began the transformation of the village from an isolated rural community to a comfortable commuter suburb.

Richard and his father-in-law were prominent in business in the village through the activities of the brewery. Gradually, amalgamations and closures would make these small breweries a thing of the past. In 1872, a sad and unexpected event brought about changes in the Parr and Daft families. On 16 March, Butler Parr died. He left his widow, Ann, and their two children, Mary Daft, who was 30 years of age, and Butler Parr junior, who was only 13. After making provision for his wife, he left the bulk of his estate between his two children equally. He was careful to circumvent the law which provided that a married woman's assets should belong to her husband: young Butler Parr's share would be

Brewery House, Walker's Yard, Radcliffe-on-Trent,
now converted from its earlier use.

held in trust for him until he was 21. Someone saw the possibility of conflict over the shares in the brewery, leading to one of the joint owners having to buy out the other, which would place Richard, appointed as executor and trustee, in an impossible position; in the event, he did not join in obtaining probate of the will. As a result of the terms of the will, Richard still acted only as manager of the brewery, and as the seventies wore on, he may have felt his young brother-in-law's beady eye observing the activity there while half of the profits were invested elsewhere on his behalf.

Richard must have felt the need for some diversions, and one of them was football. In the 1830s the game was rough and ready, but by the 1860s it was better organised; it was taken up by some public schools and carried into afterlife by their old boys. In 1862, a group of young lawyers, bankers and other professional men decided to meet regularly for practice in the hollow of The Park in Nottingham. Two years later, they held a meeting at the George Hotel, when sixteen enthusiasts resolved that 'a football club be established for this county and that it shall be named the Notts Football Club.' The principal pioneers were Mr F.C.Smith, Major Hack, Mr R.Daft and others. They dressed in amber and black jerseys and had rare matches among the members.

This was further confirmation of Richard's social standing among amateur sportsmen in his age group at the age of 28. His first match for the team, by now named Notts County, was on 2 January, 1865 against Sheffield, and he went on to appear pretty regularly for them up to the end of 1871. Most of their matches were played in The Meadows and the names of some of their opponents are familiar – Lincoln, Sheffield and Chesterfield. He referred in *Kings of Cricket* to very rough play. Hacking, tripping and elbowing were all acceptable. Players could charge the goal-keeper – even if he was nowhere near the ball! Richard remained an enthusiastic supporter of the side throughout his life, and all the more so after his son, Harry, joined the side.

Another diversion which gave Richard great enjoyment was boxing. He had been a practitioner himself, learning the craft from a professional lightweight called Patsy Clay. Richard often met Ben Caunt, a champion of his generation and a Notts man. 'He stood about 6ft 3in and must, when I was acquainted with him, have weighed 18 or 19 stone. A grim and battered warrior was Ben. He dressed very elaborately, having two or three rings on his fingers and wearing a jewelled scarf pin of large dimensions.' Richard himself was rather smaller than Caunt; in 1865 he reported himself as 5ft 9in tall and 10st 6lb in weight. He often saw Tom Sayers and Jem Mace, but the one who made the most impression on him was William 'Bendigo' Thompson, one of the most famous sportsmen to come from Nottingham. 'He possessed a head of adamantine hardness and would allow any man to give him a hit on the back of the head with his fist as hard as he liked. The striker who took him at his word was always a good deal more hurt.' The Australian city of Bendigo is said to have been named after him. Their bare-knuckle prize fights were illegal and held in out of the way spots, and sometimes fights went on for as long as 93 rounds.

We have already touched on Richard's hunting, shooting and fishing in his free and easy youth, but lacrosse became a passion of his following its introduction into Britain around 1880, and he took very enthusiastically to lawn tennis. One cannot imagine anyone taking less than the keenest interest in any activity they were sharing with him. There were, in addition, according to *Scores and Biographies*, boating, billiards and cycling, while he enjoyed a day at the races in congenial company. Later on he offered games of skittles and bowling to visitors to The Rosery, his house, which lies just across Walker's Yard from the brewery.

The Daft family home, The Rosery, at Radcliffe-on-Trent in 2007: it is now used by a local Scout group.

Chapter Ten
More of the County Championship

Cricket always remained to the fore. In 1872, Richard played in one match more than in the previous season and, in all first-class matches, scored 589 runs at an average of 34.64. John Selby had an even finer summer. The county's performance was not strong: they won only two matches and drew the remaining five, but the press consensus, if one can be deduced, was that they had 'retained first place' among the counties. The reasons for the decline in the number of wins were clear to see. Alfred Shaw soon became too ill to play and because of injury Biddulph, the wicket-keeper, could turn out only twice. The lack of a good man behind the stumps was an enormous handicap to the remaining bowlers. Jemmy Shaw declined as a member of the attack, but this was not the disadvantage it might have been as it led to the introduction into the side of Fred Morley, fast left-arm. Of Morley, Daft's opinion was 'if he bowled like a machine, he certainly resembled a machine that was well oiled and in perfect working order.' They were however the best county batting side, scoring 20.89 runs per wicket, higher than any of their rivals.

Richard himself went from strength to strength after an unpromising start. He was a member of the United North Eleven, who at the end of April were dismissed for totals of 46 and 68 by the United South at the Wavertree Road Ground, Edge Hill, Liverpool - the predecessor of the Aigburth enclosure. His own innings totalled 14 and 13: he failed in his first county match of the season against Yorkshire at Trent Bridge, although Notts won the match. So, when, in the following week, he was bowled at Lord's for nought in the first innings against the Gentlemen, there were not wanting critics to suggest that he was getting past his prime.

The next morning, Richard read a piece by W.H.Knight, the editor of *Wisden* and a well-known sporting journalist, that made him cross. According to Knight, he had lost all form and at his time of life, 36, he ought not to have been chosen for the big match. When the Players went in for the second time, in a minority of 51, they increased their advantage to a lead of only six for the loss of two wickets as Daft advanced to the wicket at 1.40 pm. During Richard's partnership with Ephraim Lockwood, *Wisden* recorded that one over from Powys played by Daft 'deservedly elicited a ringing shout of applause, the "well bowled" and "well played" being equally merited.' Later, Bob Carpenter and Daft mastered the attack. At 225, Carpenter was caught when Richard's total was 92: it was not encouraging that John Smith, Pooley and McIntyre all fell cheaply, but by the time Richard was bowled off his glove at 238, he had scored a chanceless 102. He departed to a 'hearty prolonged shout of applause'. He had hit one 5 and ten fours. W.G., who had scored 77 in his first innings, hit up 112 in 127 minutes in the second, enabling the Gentlemen to win comfortably by seven wickets. After his own dismissal, Richard advised Knight to be more careful before asserting that a cricketer was not worthy of his place.

W.G. was again conspicuous in the next match, which was between the same teams at The Oval. In the follow-on, the Players were subsiding at 80 for five wickets when Richard and Pooley, the wicket-keeper, made a stand. They were aided by W.G., who dropped Richard and then converted an off-drive for five by him, all run, into a nine by an overthrow. When he had scored 27, a ball from Brice hurt Richard so severely that he had to retire. He missed the Yorkshire match at Trent Bridge, and in Notts' next home match against Surrey, he failed and may still not have been fit. Luckily, this was certainly not so when W.G. and Gloucestershire were the next visitors. The match was watched over the three days by nearly 20,000 people. Many had come to see W.G. but Notts batted from the start of the match at 12.35 on the Thursday until 6 pm the following evening! After Oscroft and Wyld put on 91 for the second wicket, Wyld joined by Richard added another 91 runs for the third wicket. When Wyld was bowled with the total on 183, there was only a temporary respite before Richard, now joined by Selby, saw the Notts total up by a further 87. Richard was at last caught at 270: he accumulated 33 singles and only three fours in his 84. Selby was undefeated for 128 – only the second hundred for Notts at Trent Bridge. The crowd saw plenty of W.G. as he bowled 89 four-ball overs to take seven wickets for 162, and on the last day he scored 67 out of the Gloucester total of 139. On his dismissal, his team's batting and interest in the match evaporated.

So on to Canterbury for North versus South, where after brilliant fielding on the part of the North, Richard was greeted with cheers as he advanced to the wicket – but it was 23 minutes before he got off the mark. He and Carpenter gradually built up a stand of 113. The man of the day was James Lillywhite junior, the Sussex left-arm bowler, and rather later, England captain, who captured all the North wickets for 129. Richard was caught behind by Pooley with his score on 64. Against Surrey, his innings reached 78, earned by three and a half hours of 'cautious' and 'scientific' cricket 'such as but few other batsmen can play,' in the words of *Wisden*. At 55 for seven, Richard, in second wicket down, had already been in for 69 minutes for his score of 12. Later, Martin McIntyre successfully assailed the Surrey attack. The score had climbed to 202 when Richard was out. His innings again included 33 singles, as well as 4 fours. In contrast, McIntyre slammed his 88 with the aid of a five and 7 fours. Notts then put Surrey out for 60 and they followed on, eventually setting Notts 167 to win. At the close, they in turn had struggled to reach 107 for eight, Richard being caught for only three.

At Sheffield the following week, he scored 27 and 21 not out to save the game for Notts, who after being set 170 for victory, just scraped a draw at 81 for seven. In the Yorkshire second innings, Richard bowled 37 overs of lobs and ended with six wickets for 59, the best return of his first-class career.

A week later, at Clifton, he had the better of the home attack which lacked W.G., who was preparing to tour Canada. First, the two other famous Graces, E.M. and G.F., hit hundreds in Gloucester-shire's total of 317. The weather was superb and the attendance large when Notts began their innings. Richard went in at number four and steadied the helm when Notts were struggling with the score at 54 for 4: only Barnes stayed in with him to add 50, and by close of play Notts had struggled to 179 for 8, with Richard on 61. Little was expected of their remaining batsmen, Morley and J.C.Shaw, when the game resumed next day before a crowd of 8,000. Following the cheap dismissal of Morley, Jemmy Shaw proceeded to play the innings of his life, defending stubbornly for an hour and forty minutes, while Richard increased his own total to 92, in the process saving the follow-on. At last, Shaw was bowled for nine with the total at 239. Richard himself had batted for five hours, hit five fours and run 47 singles. In *Kings of Cricket* he wrote that on the morning of that third day, he learned that Notts would have to bat a man short because Shaw had, the previous evening, got quarrelling at cards and rushed out saying he would 'go and do for himself'. Daft's thoughts turned to the Clifton Suspension Bridge, and it was a great relief when Frank Townsend, one of the Gloucestershire players, reported that he had seen an object lying under a tree on the Downs, which proved to be Jemmy Shaw. Gloucestershire, unable to enforce the follow-on, batted out time.

W.G. was easily first in the batting averages, with 1,485 runs at the grand average of 57.11. Richard, scoring 589 at 34.64, went to the wicket 20 times compared with Grace's 29 innings. For many years the convention among cricket historians was that the starting year for the competition was 1873, on the ground that in that year the regulations governing the qualification of players were first applied, but for those participating or watching at the time, 1873 was no different from 1872.

Richard was afflicted by quinsy (a throat infection) in the spring of 1873, but recovered in time for the start of the season. Notts faced a number of improbable incidents: Alfred Shaw had recovered from illness but was injured when a powder flask exploded. Then the two fixtures with Gloucestershire were scrapped; W.G. had committed himself to play in a benefit match which clashed with one of the games between his county and Notts, and when the Notts committee found that the champion, who was notably supportive of professional benefits, wanted the date of the county meeting changed, they inexplicably refused to play Gloucestershire at all.

Two other matches also gave rise to controversy: the Huddersfield Club asked Richard personally to take a Notts team to play a Yorkshire side. The affair turned out disastrously for the visitors, as the hosts scored 194 while the wicket was playing easily: heavy rain then totally changed the conditions and Notts were bundled out twice. G.B.Davy, their secretary, tried to repair the damage to the club's reputation by writing to the press explaining that the game was an unofficial one, but the papers still insisted on treating the result as a championship loss for Notts. This was a decisive factor in the county having to share the top place with Gloucestershire instead of heading the list.

Even more unpalatable was Notts' match against the lowly Derbyshire team, which was played in September. This was a clear case of pride coming before a fall, as Notts insisted on allowing the opposition sixteen players. Derbyshire mustered 114 before dismissing the great Notts eleven for only 14 and going on to defeat Notts by an innings.

Turning to happier events, Richard opened the season against Yorkshire at Trent Bridge with the highest innings he ever played in a first-class match – although he was to exceed it by a long way as late as 1885, but not in first-class company. In splendid weather, the two Shaws put out their opponents for 65. The Notts total was 42 for two when Richard went to the wicket. Bignall was next out at 83 before the entry of Martin McIntyre, who hit up 48 out of 71 for the fourth partnership. Richard played very finely to reach 80, and with Selby on 29 had taken Notts' reply to 228 for four by close of play. The brilliant part of his innings came on the second day. Richard, joined by Biddulph with the score at 270 for seven, was soon in his best form, hitting, according to *Wisden*, in such brilliant and telling style that they had taken the total to 333 when Biddulph was run out. Morley stayed in until 355, when, attempting a big hit to leg, Richard was caught by long-stop! His 161, out of 313, was as fine a display of first-class hitting as was seen in 1873. This, the highest innings yet played at Trent Bridge, Richard amassed with the aid of eighteen fours and as many as 45 singles. It was the highest first-class score for the county until Shrewsbury's 207 versus Surrey at The Oval in 1882. The previous Notts record was George Parr's 130, also versus Surrey at The Oval, in 1859. Years later, Louis Hall of Yorkshire, whose first season this was, told *Old Ebor*: 'I had the pleasure of seeing Richard Daft get 161 against Yorkshire at Trent Bridge. To use a favourite expression of Tom Emmett, it was like playing with the sharp edge of a knife. He also made that beautiful leg stroke of his; I never saw anything to equal it.' On his return to the dressing room, Daft was greeted with an ovation and summoned to the pavilion for a presentation by the Notts committee, who awarded him the largest award of talent money they had ever made. Yorkshire followed with 170, so Notts were victorious by an innings and 120 runs.

His century apart, Richard's only score over fifty in county matches came against Surrey at The Oval. Notts played a very settled side in which ten players appeared in every match. Alfred Shaw, at the age of 31, came into his own. His victims in Nottinghamshire's fixtures numbered 43, at an average of 11.09. In all matches, his figures were: 1,357.3 overs, 656 maidens, 1,675 runs, and 121 wickets, average 13.84.

Richard's record for that season shows what a small amount of first-class cricket he was playing. The same was not true of W.G., although Gloucestershire's county matches were limited to six. In his eight first-class matches, Richard's figures were 416 runs at 41.60, while those of W.G., in twenty matches, showed 1,805 runs, including six centuries, at an average of 72.20. The Great Man, who was 25 years old by the end of the season, also captured 75 wickets. He also played pretty well a full season for the United South Eleven in their matches against odds. The consensus was that the title of champion county for 1873 was shared between Gloucestershire and Notts.

Chapter Eleven
Gentlemen and Players

Before the season of 1874, Richard suffered a commercial disaster. Since 1868, he had become well-established as a sports outfitter in Lister Gate, Nottingham, with H.A.Finn as his manager. When his employer censured him for negligence and inattention to business, Finn immediately gave a fortnight's notice. Most employees would have made him leave at once and looked for a replacement, but this did not occur to Richard. A day or two later, Finn left a note for him with the errand boy saying that he had been unexpectedly called to Liverpool for a discussion about a new job. In fact, he had absconded with the takings. The police also suspected forgery and took out a warrant for Finn's arrest. Armed with the warrant, a detective travelled to Liverpool where Finn had family, drawing

Continuity. Daft's sports warehouse on the corner of Lister Gate, Nottingham occupied premises built in 1854:
the building remains in shop use and even sells sports outfits, of a sort.

blank with them; he traced a payment from the address in Nottingham of Finn's girlfriend towards the fare for the two of them to New York. Alas, Finn and his girl had sailed the previous day, escaping the jurisdiction of English law.

This was a bad example to a young employee whom Richard had taken on as a fourteen-year-old two years before. The youth would later become a highly successful rival to Richard in business as well as a member of Notts and England elevens. His name was William Gunn.

This season, 1874, was a rare one when Notts were let down by their batsmen, with the result that they lost six of their ten first-class matches. Only Richard, still at the head of the averages with 370 runs, but at an average of no more than 21.76, showed anything like first-class batting, and it was a long time before he achieved much. He scored 43 for Notts against Surrey in a low-scoring match at Trent Bridge at the end of June. A week later he made two good efforts for the Players at Lord's, but his 43 in the first innings occupied 100 minutes, 12 of his first 14 runs being singles, and his 19 in the second engaged, if that is the word, the spectators for 80 minutes. His side would have been hard put to it without him when they went in a second time to score 161 to win: they reached their goal by two wickets. The Gentlemen may have been irked, not only by the result but by the way Richard chose to play the slow left-arm bowler, David Buchanan, who over after over, tossed the ball up outside the off stump. In his own words: 'Daft, though he played a very good innings, allowed some 20 off balls in succession from me to go past him without attempting to play them.'

But there was a further edge to the feeling between some Gentlemen and some Players. On 10 June 1874, the day after the finish of the match at Lord's between MCC and Notts, the London correspondent of the *Nottingham Journal* mused: 'The little cricket quarrel does not appear to have been made up yet. Daft will not play, it seems, in the same matches as Mr G. [*sic*] Grace so long as that cricketer continues to rank as a "gentleman", while he, Daft, is reckoned only a "player". For this, there is some show of reason. Daft was once a "gentleman player" but his means being somewhat circumscribed, he was fain to take the salary of a player, and as such had to figure in the matches without the prefix "Mr" to his name, and to associate with the other professionals.'

The correspondent continued: 'Mr Grace, [Richard] states, receives a salary and yet is allowed to call himself a gentleman player and to have wine with his lunch, while Daft sits with the professionals and has beer. Of course, all this is very galling to the distinguished Nottingham cricketer, and he may be excused for feeling a little hurt at the difference . . . but in the interests of the game, it is a pity that two such accomplished opponents should not meet at the wickets and defeat each other there. Daft is certainly the next best all-round man to Grace, but he is not the leviathan and he will scarcely succeed in increasing his reputation by the means he has adopted.'

Three days later, under the heading 'MR R DAFT AND THE CRICKET FEUD', the *Journal* resumed: 'Our London Correspondent's gossiping remarks about the "little cricket quarrel" have caused some discussion in cricketing circles. . . . The statement that Daft "was once a gentleman player . . ." applies with as much, if not more, force to Grace. He, as is well-known, plays in matches the whole season through for the sake of the "salary". Daft, on the contrary, only plays occasionally, his ordinary business engagements being of far more importance to him than any salary of a player. It is the very fact of Daft's non-appearance at most of the principal matches in the country, from the above cause, which is put down to a refusal on his part to play in the same matches as Grace.'

Up to the second week in June 1874, there had been only three matches in which Richard and W.G. could have met. Richard did not appear in any of them: he was playing for Notts against Sixteen of Derbyshire on the same dates as the first, North versus South beginning on 25 May, but did not have any first-class or important cricket engagements to coincide with the others. He had five further opportunities to engage with W.G. that summer, and took part in two of them – for Players versus Gentlemen at Lord's early in July, when he scored 43 and 19, and in the repeat match at Prince's when W.G. dismissed him twice, for 21 and 0. Looking back to the previous year, Richard had turned out on 15 May for North versus South at Prince's, but he let seven other chances of a meeting slip, and the two did not face each other again that summer. Only once was Richard playing elsewhere when he might have been playing Grace. Significantly, when he failed to represent the North at The Oval on 24 July 1873, his previous game had been for Notts at the same venue on the immediately preceding days.

So, the *Journal's* man had some grounds for gossiping as he did on 10 June, 1874 - Richard had missed ten fixtures in succession against W.G. In fact, Richard played fewer first-class innings in 1873 than in any season since 1863. In 1874, he went to the crease almost twice as frequently as in the previous year - 21 innings as against twelve. Yet, we should still remember the extent of his business responsibilities, the brewery and the sports shop, and his realisation, following his manager's dishonesty, of the need to have a presence everywhere. Then his family was increasing: by 1874, Richard Parr Daft was ten years old and Harry was eight. There were now two daughters as well - Ann was two, while Mary was born that year.

One cannot avoid the events of the match at Prince's between the Gentlemen and Players beginning 23 July, 1874. We have already noted that W.G. twice dismissed Richard in that game. Richard cannot have been very thrilled at the controversial newspaper articles, even if he had done nothing to provoke them. The Players led on the first innings by 21, but then W.G. ran away with the match by fair means and foul - by his transcendent all-round play and his gamesmanship. In the second innings, he attacked from the start. Fred Grace joined him with the total already at 129 for two. Before Fred had scored, he played the ball back to the bowler, James Lillywhite, who could have made an easy catch had not W.G. been 'palpably in the way'. Lillywhite appealed to both umpires for obstruction of the field by W.G., but they both turned down the appeal. This was received with incredulity by the Players and brought to a head their dissatisfaction with the umpires. As *Wisden* put it: 'It was their misfortune in this match that nearly every appeal by the Gentlemen was decided affirmatively and the Players' appeals were mainly met with not out.'

On the third day, W.G. completed his hundred, leaving the Players 189 to win. Whether or not the two umpires, George Keeble and Alfred Luff, with previous first-class experience of one match each, were influenced by the overwhelming presence and personality of W.G., they soon had an influence on the result. Richard was given out lbw for a duck and Charlwood soon followed, caught behind, both vigorously protesting against the decisions: the Players were all out for 128. *Wisden's* comment was that 'the decisions of these two young umpires were conscientious, no doubt, but that they are yet too inexperienced for office in a match of such high class is equally certain.'

Richard was now in his 39th year. W.G's birthday on 18 July, 1874 was his 26th. For nearly ten years, he had stood beyond all comparison with his contemporaries. The question of his status was, as we have seen, already becoming a matter of public discussion. The Grace family were not gentry or heirs to wealth. With his county, W.G. reached an understanding by which he was paid expenses well beyond the money he actually spent in playing the game. He also took the profit from the activities of the United South of England Eleven.

In the autumn of 1873, he married and for their honeymoon took his wife on a cricket tour of Australia. Melbourne Cricket Club agreed to pay him £1,500 and first-class travel and expenses for himself and his wife. The team was to be a mix of amateurs and professionals: W.G. offered the latter second-class passage, £150 pay for the trip and £20 spending money. From first to last, W.G. insisted on complete social segregation between his not very distinguished amateur colleagues and the professional members of his team: he turned down any social invitations which included the professionals. The Australians, with their claims to social equality, were quick to notice W.G's segregationism. A columnist wrote: 'The consequence of this is what might be expected – insubordination in the ranks, a divided team, and humiliating defeats . . .'

The team were back in England by 17 May, 1874. W.G. celebrated by hitting up 259 for Thornbury against Clifton on 21 May. William Oscroft had been in W.G.'s side and he and Richard did not play together until Notts met MCC at Lord's on 8 and 9 June, when their reunion can hardly have taken place without a discussion of the tour.

Then on Wednesday, 10 June, that piece of gossip appeared in the *Nottingham Journal*. Was the story an invention of the columnist? It was more likely an echo of the comments of the pros in the touring party, passed on by Oscroft to Richard. W.G's machinations had already been going on for years, and must have touched a raw nerve of Richard's in 1874.

While on the topic of raw nerves, two defeats by Yorkshire, the first in June at Trent Bridge and the other at Sheffield in August, cannot have improved the captain's temper. Nor can the observations of the *Nottingham Journal* reporter, following the June match. The phrases thundered off the page: 'Inglorious defeat'; 'We shall lose much of our prestige . . .'; 'We were defeated in the earlier part of the week by the Marylebone Cricket Club and we have been thrashed out of time by the Yorkshire men . . . '; 'Never have we seen Nottingham cricket to so great a disadvantage . . .'

Such failure was not really offset by Richard's innings of 102 against the weak Sussex attack at Trent Bridge, nor by a comfortable victory over the Southerners by an innings. Richard had batted for two and three quarter hours, making his runs out of 194 and hitting 12 fours, yet in the return fixture at Hove, Sussex emerged as easy winners, Richard making one and nought. It was their only victory of the season.

At the end of the season of 1874, G.B.Davy, the county's Honorary Secretary, resigned. The formidable Captain Henry Holden, Chief Constable of the Nottingham Town Police, succeeded him. Holden, who came from long-established gentry in Derbyshire, was also Honorary Treasurer of the club until 1882. He took no hostages and operated on a very short fuse. If these characteristics worked successfully in managing the Constabulary, they were sometimes ineffective in his relationships with the professional cricketers. Yet he and Richard worked happily together. The comfortable nature of their association, observed by the other members of the side, laid the seeds of dissension after Richard's retirement from the county team.

Meanwhile, in 1875, Nottinghamshire made a complete return to their best form and were generally considered to be champion county. They played two matches each with Yorkshire, Surrey, Gloucestershire, Middlesex and Derbyshire, and contended with MCC at Lord's: of these matches they won six and lost two. The team underwent changes. Out went Jemmy Shaw, Biddulph and Bignall. Incomers included William Barnes and Arthur Shrewsbury. The latter, then aged nineteen, would become the finest professional batsman of his generation, and Barnes developed into an all-rounder of international stature. The effect of these changes was to strengthen the side which now comprised William Oscroft, Fred Wyld, William Barnes, Richard Daft, John Selby, Arthur Shrewsbury, Martin McIntyre, Henry Reynolds, William Clark, Alfred Shaw and Fred Morley. These last two dominated the bowling – Shaw had 82 victims in 1875, Morley 36 – and were well supported by William Clarke, of Old Basford, and McIntyre. How long would Richard retain his place in this renowned side?

Richard Daft himself had only a moderate time: he showed a distinct decline with the bat, while many observers found him less certain and effective in the field. As to his captaincy, he had only to wind up Alfred Shaw at one end to gain control of the opposing batsmen: every man knew his place in the field, and the team batted all the way down to number nine.

But there were times when things went irretrievably wrong. The team's only defeat by a county – they also lost to MCC – came at the hands of Yorkshire at Trent Bridge right at the end of the season. *Wisden* described the matches between these two counties as 'The Battle of the Bowlers' and so this match confirmed. Shaw and Morley scattered the visitors for 49 on the first day: Notts fared better, Daft 13 and Shrewsbury 29 not out being the principal contributors to Notts' total of 87. In their second innings, the Yorkshire men gave a greatly improved performance. *Wisden* thought that Shaw and Morley were badly supported in the field: Notts began to slip, and at the close of the second day they were 3 for three. *Wisden* commented briskly: 'On the third day, the attendance was slack, the cricket brief, and the end a frightful fiasco for Notts.' At 25 for four, the umpire decided long-stop, Thewlis, had caught out Daft. The umpire was Cornelius Coward. Notts declined to 58 all out to give Yorkshire victory by 87 runs.

Back to the match between the same counties at Sheffield at the end of May, which Notts went on to win comfortably. In pleasant weather, each side had completed an innings by the end of the first day – Yorkshire 89, Notts 84. On the second day, Yorkshire's dismissal for 107 left Notts 112 to win. Their openers, Wyld and William Oscroft took the score to 12, when Wyld played a delivery from Allan Hill to mid-off, Ullathorne. He returned the ball to Pinder, the wicket-keeper, who tossed it up to Hill. Hill, seeing that Oscroft had not regained his crease, put down the wicket: the umpire, Coward, gave Oscroft out. Oscroft protested vehemently, but unavailingly, and walked off the ground, accompanied by Wyld, and was followed after an interval by the fielding side. A delay of half an hour occurred – the spectators overflowed onto the ground demanding a resumption of play. At length, of course, common sense prevailed and Oscroft had to go. As *The Times* put it: 'The whole thing hangs on whether the ball was finally settled in the wicket-keeper's hands or not. The Yorkshire men aver that Pinder received a signal from Allan Hill to shy it over and he threw the ball with the intention of running Oscroft out. Coward was the only one to judge and his decision, right or wrong, should have been respected.' *'Green Lilly'* later criticised Richard for failing to control the Notts players during this incident.

Richard's only innings of note for the county was 47 against Gloucestershire at Trent Bridge at the end of July. With Selby, Richard put on 69 which won the match for Notts. Even then W.G. caused his opponents some qualms: he took four of the six wickets to fall, including that of Richard, who went in to bat with 17 to win. It was 7.20 pm: no doubt Richard intended to finish off the match that evening, but W.G., sticking when it suited him, to the strict letter of the law refused to finish the match – after all, it might rain overnight. It didn't, and Notts shuffled to victory next day in 40 minutes, Richard contributing four before being caught and bowled – by W.G.

He batted better in the two great matches in which he turned out in London. The first was for Notts against MCC at Lord's in June. Yet, even when he did well, there was a patronising tone in the reports: 'Daft appeared somewhat nervous on commencing his first innings, and it was sometime before he settled down. ... His 25 runs ... were not made in his old form, but in his second innings he quickly got into something like it, saw seven wickets fall, and took out his bat.' Richard's scores of 25 and 35 not out were excellent in a low-scoring match, but the real hero was Alfred Shaw whose second-innings figures were seven wickets for seven runs; nevertheless, MCC were successful by 62 runs.

On 5 July, 1875, at Lord's, Richard for the first time captained the Players against the Gentlemen. Batting second, the Players led by 17 on the first innings. When he went in to bat 'Daft was greeted with a hearty cheer. He played the remaining three balls (chippers) of Mr. Francis' over in good form.' Among those in the field was Lord Harris. He recorded how Richard's first two balls were two rasping shooters which he successfully stopped. He went on to score 28 before hitting his wicket, but the Players were overwhelmed by W.G.'s score of 152 in the Gentlemen's second innings of 444. Later, Richard fell to A.W. Ridley for a duck, as W.G. completed 12 wickets in the match, which produced a hiding for the Players by 262 runs. Later on, in September, he captained North versus South at Loughborough: his side won by 125 runs, despite W.G. taking fourteen wickets in the match.

But Richard's year had a happier ending. On 13 December, at the Annual General Meeting of the Notts County Club, it was announced that 'a complimentary benefit would be given to Mr. Richard Daft' under the management of the Committee who 'will direct the form of the testimonial to be raised by such benefit match.'

Nottinghamshire's side in 1875,
acclaimed as champion county by the contemporary press.
Standing (l to r): W.Shrewsbury, S.Biddulph (wk), H.Nixon (umpire), M.McIntyre,
R.Daft (captain), J.West (umpire), J.C.Shaw and W.Oscroft. Seated: A.Shaw,
J.Selby and F.Wyld. On the ground: F.Morley and A.Shrewsbury.

Chapter Twelve
Benefit in Kind

For cricketers in 1876, the continuous sunshine came as a strong contrast to the summers that had preceded it. The hard wickets were exactly to the taste of W.G., whose record was extraordinary. In 26 matches he scored 2,622 runs at 62.42, with only two other batsmen – Ephraim Lockwood of Yorkshire and Harry Jupp of Surrey – reaching a thousand runs. In this season, Grace held more catches than any other player, including the wicket-keepers, and took more wickets than every other bowler apart from Alfred Shaw.

Richard was fifth in the batting averages of those who played regularly. He played more first-class cricket this season than in any other and reached his highest run aggregate. Often opening the batting – he had typically batted at three, four or five before this season – he scored 976 runs in eighteen first-class matches, at an average of 34.85.

In contrast, Notts' performances were moderate, so they finished third in the championship, with four victories to set against three defeats. As always, their attack, Shaw and Morley, was formidable, but the support bowlers did not provide sufficient contrast. The county's batsmen did not give Richard much support, apart from the up-and-coming Arthur Shrewsbury, with 460 runs at an average of 27.05, and to a lesser extent, Oscroft, 379 at 23.11. Richard, at the age of 41, was the best professional batsman of the year. A season which turned out to be full of unusual incidents began with an unexpected feat with the ball by Richard, who captured six wickets in the annual Colts' match, including a hat trick. A month passed before Notts' first county match against Lancashire at Trent Bridge. In Notts' first innings, Richard hit up 70 in an excellent display of scientific batting. Forty-four was the next highest score in the match, but after the visitors had achieved a lead of 40 on the first innings, they routed Notts for 128, leaving themselves only 89 to get. For the All England Eleven against the United South of England at Lord's and in two fixtures called North versus South, Richard's total did not reach 30. At Lord's again, where MCC were hosts to Notts, Richard 'hit much freer than usual', with a six, a five and four fours in his 49.

Up to the end of June, Notts had played only one county match. At this stage came Yorkshire to Trent Bridge, and Richard, so appropriately in his benefit year, began a purple patch. He opened the innings with Arthur Shrewsbury, and both men, taking their time, began by scoring 60 in the first hour. By lunch, they had moved the total to 130, with Shrewsbury on 78 not out and Richard on 46. In the afternoon they played fluently on until, at 183, Clayton hit Richard's middle stump. The partnership had lasted three hours ten minutes and was, at the time, the highest for the county for any wicket. In his 81 he had hit six fours, six threes and 29 singles. Shrewsbury took his score to 118, but the innings subsided to 298 all out. Yorkshire's response left the home side 100 minutes to get 86 runs. Mystery hangs over Notts' performance of their mission. Shrewsbury was stumped at 23 and Oscroft and William Barnes followed. Richard himself batted an hour for only 12, and then Notts played out time with 29 runs for victory. What had stopped them in their tracks? The answer lies perhaps in the minutes of the Yorkshire Committee, who resolved 'that £1 be given to each [Yorkshire] player for the determined stand they made at Nottingham where the match was drawn': further, 'a sum of £5 should be subscribed to Richard Daft's benefit match.' Entraining south for The Oval, he captained the Players against the Gentlemen. Summer weather and the usual excellent Kennington wickets favoured the match, and 16,000 spectators were present over the three days. Richard's score reached 48, joint top scorer, and the Players totalled 237. After Emmett bowled W.G. for nought, they gained a lead of only eight; Richard again played admirably to top-score with 61, and the Gentlemen finished with six wickets to fall and 65 runs to get.

At Lord's, when the two sides met again, W.G. had things all his own way, amassing 169 in the Gentlemen's total of 449. In reply, the Players could not get enough runs in the face of their inexorable opponent, who also had nine wickets in the match, which the Gentlemen won by an innings and 98 runs. Richard did his bit, scoring 28 as opening bat and going in lower down next time, finishing undefeated on 39. A week later, Middlesex entertained Notts, who had much the best of the match, enforcing the follow-on and needing only 55 to win: yet, this match, too, finished inconclusively. The Prince's ground-keeper, Tom Box, a famous wicket-keeper in former days, collapsed while on duty on the scoreboard and died. The match was at once abandoned. Richard had shown some fine hitting for 82 in Notts' first innings. Lancashire provided much tougher opposition at Old Trafford where Notts just held on for a draw. Richard's visits to the crease brought him totals of only four and nine; the following fixture was in all probability engaging his concentration.

The Committee had decided that his testimonial should take the form of a match between North and South at Nottingham and the start date, 17 July, was now imminent. Robert Thoms, the best-known umpire of the day, who stood in Richard's match, wrote:

> On making tracks for the 'Old Trent Bridge' ground, on the Monday morning, I was struck by the commotion then apparent in the town, and also by the stream of pedestrians and vehicles heavy laden making their way in the same direction; and by the time wickets had been pitched and the ball set rolling, the visitors thus early had taken up all the available seats and best positions for viewing the game, whilst by the dinner-hour the gathering had increased by thousands. I have, during the past twenty years, been planted in some big rings, but never before saw a more densely-packed and enthusiastic body of spectators, the din of whose voices filled the air with an incessant hum; and it is a question if a better attendance has ever been seen at a great match for three consecutive days, either in or out of London.

The greatest compliment to Richard was provided by the quality of the two sides as shown on the scorecard, which appears at Appendix Two to this book. The South, in spite of an early collapse, led by 53 on the first innings, but it was anybody's match when by consistent batting (A.N.Hornby 44, Richard 38, R.P.Smith of Derbyshire 39, Ephraim Lockwood 57 not out) the North left their opponents 190 runs to win in 210 minutes – anybody's match, that is, but for W.G. First, he and Webbe took apart the attack to the tune of 100 in 66 minutes, and after the dismissal of Webbe, W.G. did as he liked, hitting 114 out of 190 for two in two hours twenty-five minutes. He had given two chances – the first to Richard at long-on. On Monday 5,839 attended; on Tuesday 6,673; and on Wednesday 3,445, with the turnstile takings amounting to £398 18s 6d, and another £40 14s 0d for admission to the pavilion.

Money came in from other sources: MCC £25, the Notts Club £25, and many others, and also gifts of silver.

A week later, Notts entertained Gloucestershire at Trent Bridge. This was one of the visitors' finest seasons, and their all-amateur team was unbeaten up to this match; they remained undefeated at the season's end. W.G. had a wonderful time for the county, amassing 890 runs in 11 completed innings, and he received such support from his colleagues that Gloucestershire won this match comfortably by six wickets. Richard continued his good form, scoring 35 and 30, but Notts' lead of 10 on the first innings was not enough: they collapsed to 97 in their second. W.G. made all the difference: his 60 in Gloucestershire's first effort was remarkable. Until he was finely caught at point by Oscroft, when the Gloucester score stood at only 75, he had not given a semblance of a chance.

Notts' next opponents were Surrey, who were easily defeated by 10 wickets; Richard's contribution was 24 in the first innings. To score only four for the United North against the United South at Anlaby Road, Hull, was a disappointment, particularly when W.G. followed 126 in his first innings with 82 in the second. Notts were to see much more of him yet. After a ten-day break, they took the train south to Bristol where, on the Clifton College ground, he humbled them. Gloucestershire totalled 400 – W.G. 177: Notts, 265 and 165, just avoided an innings defeat, as W.G. ensnared eight of them for 69 in the second attempt. Richard (62) and Oscroft (84) made a splendid response in an opening stand of 151, but otherwise only John Tye, with 48 in the second innings, made much of a show.

Their demolition was enlivened by what *'Green Lilly'* regretted to report as an unpleasant incident, in which 'the only amateur playing for Notts [was] most unwarrantably assailed with language, the very reverse of gentlemanly by one who should have known very much better.' This arose after Tolley, the Notts amateur, took a single off W.G.: the fielder missed the wicket and they ran an overthrow. The report continues: 'Unhappily, the gentleman amateur (Tolley) tried to hit the overthrow ball as it passed him but did not succeed; G.F. appealed for hitting the ball twice, but it was turned down as the ball had not been hit.' There was then two minutes' play left that evening. Tolley put his bat down and stooped to adjust his pads: he took so long over this that W.G. swore at him.

Bell's Life referred to an exciting scene when stumps were drawn for the day: 'The umpires drew stumps and Tolley was justly cheered for resenting the ungentlemanly behaviour. It is to be hoped that such a scene as this will never again be witnessed on a cricket ground, especially when one side is <u>composed entirely of amateurs</u>.'

Notts made their deflated way to Temple Meads Station, bound for home. On the platform they found the Yorkshire team just arrived to take on Gloucestershire. 'I'll shoot W.G.' said Tom Emmett, 'before he takes so many runs off us.' But W.G. scored 318 not out, while his side totalled 528! That summer he had already piled up 400 not out against Twenty-two of Grimsby.

Back at Trent Bridge, Notts met Middlesex in a match played in beautiful weather and in good batting conditions, with many changes of fortune. Richard opened the match with his highest score of the season, a grand and faultless display which occupied three and a half hours: his was the ninth wicket to fall, being caught at 99. No other Notts batsman achieved more than 24 in the match. Middlesex followed on 83 behind, but fared much better and left the home side 132 to win. There then occurred another of Notts' collapses. Barnes and Tolley staved off defeat and Notts finished on 90 for eight.

After a break, Richard and his team journeyed to Bramall Lane, Sheffield for a match made remarkable by Fred Morley's bowling. Over 6,000 were present on the first day, a local holiday, in showery weather to see their side shot out for 87. The appreciative crowd then witnessed the demolition of Notts on the second day by Robert Clayton, the fast bowler; Richard's score, 16, constituted more than a third of his side's total of 46. Morley, supported by Alfred Shaw, then dismissed Yorkshire for 32, and by close of play Notts, needing 73 to win, were halfway there at 36 for one. Richard batted throughout the 77 overs bowled in that innings, and with his 39 not out and useful support from Shrewsbury and Barnes saw Notts to an eight-wicket victory on the third day.

Notts returned to Trent Bridge for another success. Early on the second day, when Richard was dismissed for 33, Notts, on 66 for one, were already 40 ahead of Surrey on the first innings! Shrewsbury, going in at No 3, scored 65 out of his side's total of 150 before Shaw and Morley bowled Surrey out for 100, leaving

Notts victors by an innings and 24 runs. Shaw took eleven for 56 and Morley nine for 45.

The proceeds of Richard's testimonial were not presented to him immediately. The County Committee announced at the club's Annual General Meeting that they had purchased a most handsome service of plate which they would present to him at the George Hotel on 11 January, 1877.

Richard's equivocal status among sportsmen was reflected in the form that the presentation took, which was generous yet gentrified. In addition to a purse of five hundred sovereigns (£37,000 in modern terms), he received a magnificent tea and coffee service, a splendid salver, a tankard (the gift of John Walker of Southgate), and from Captain Holden a hunting flask. All were of solid silver. Subsequently, Richard received, in addition, a silver sandwich case from G.B.Davy, the former secretary of the county, a dining-room clock and a pair of bronze candelabra, a fine pair of bronzes and a drawing-room clock. In the hotel dining-room, Sir Henry Bromley, President of the Nottinghamshire County Cricket Club, was in the chair, with Captain Holden on his left and Richard seated on his right. The names of the cricketers who had accepted invitations included the brightest and best of Notts' players over the previous fifty years, from Tom Barker, whose career had begun in the 1820s, and George Parr, and continuing as a roll of honour to the beneficiary. The gifts made a magnificent show, displayed in a case at the upper end of the room. On the salver the inscription read: 'Presented together with a tea and coffee service and a purse of 500 sovereigns to Richard Daft by the admirers of cricket throughout the Kingdom 1876.'

There were no fewer than fifteen speeches before Sir Henry rose to hit the right note. 'It has been said by an old heathen philosopher that the grandest sight in the world is to see a good man struggling against adversity. It might be very true, but my opinion is that if we had that old sage around us on an occasion as this one, we would soon convince him that we had an even grander sight – it was in seeing so large an assembly that night to greet a man of our own county – a man who was not only good as a cricketer, but as a citizen and one who has ingratiated himself in our good feelings.' . . . (Applause) . . . 'He had 'also a recollection of the time when I came down to meet the Nottingham Commercial Club in whose ranks I saw practising a small young lad whose defence, even then, was remarkable. He began at the beginning; he learnt defence and never left it until it was made easy to him.' . . . (Cheers) . . . 'But time went on. I saw that boy grow up into manhood, and now we have him before us as our guest tonight.' . . . 'In Richard Daft we have a model cricketer.' . . . 'Daft had been tried in the fire and not found wanting. Whether in the cricket field or in his social life, he was alike respected . . . and so it was a most gratifying thing to see him, the recipient of such a splendid testimonial tonight.' . . . (Cheers)

Sir Henry formally handed over the testimonial on behalf of the subscribers. His final gesture was to add a sealed donation from his own pocket. When the welcoming calls and applause died away, Richard replied: 'I can scarcely express my feelings on such an auspicious occasion, which I regard as the chief event of my cricket life. I feel that I am hardly in a state of mind to express sufficiently my thanks for the extraordinary honour you have done me in presenting such a magnificent testimonial.' Then an interruption from Captain Holden: 'Nothing more than is deserved.' Richard, unabashed, told his audience: 'It is true that throughout my cricket career I have endeavoured to uphold the game, whilst I have played it as keenly as possible. At the time alluded to by Sir Henry, I little thought I should occupy the honourable position in the cricket world I hope I occupy now. I felt that there was a chance of distinguishing myself for the county, which was really my ambition. As to the testimonial, I assure you I shall always regard it as an heirloom, and it will be my greatest pride to think that my children, after twenty years' connection with cricket on my part, would have something to point to and say that there was one in the family who, at any rate, attained a certain position in the cricketing world, and which position is recognised by my native county.' (Cheers) 'It is extremely pleasing to me to see gentlemen like Captain Denison and Sir Henry Bromley coming out of their way to attend such a gathering.' ('Hear, hear.') 'I feel much indebted to you, as indeed I am to all present, and so long as I can be of any use to the county, I shall certainly place my services at the disposal of the Committee.'

Richard sat down amidst a crescendo of cheering.

Chapter Thirteen
Notts Without Shaw

A notable absentee from the celebrations was Alfred Shaw, who was touring Australia and New Zealand, in the course of which he bowled the first delivery in Test cricket. Unfortunately for his county, he succumbed to bronchitis on his return and could not shake it off. His absence from the Notts team in 1877, apart from the first two matches (in which he captured 16 wickets) greatly weakened the side. As many as fifteen bowlers were tried for Notts, but the batting was also below its usual standard. Richard finished easily at the top of the batting, scoring 539 runs, but his average fell from 40 to 24. This was partly due to the prevalence of damp wickets which affected all the leading batsmen.

Richard's principal fault was continually getting out when he seemed to have settled. He did best in the season's major match, Gentlemen *v* Players at Lord's. As captain, he played a celebrated innings when the Players opened the match. In first, he saw Ephraim Lockwood, Arthur Shrewsbury and Harry Jupp dismissed cheaply. After lunch, 18 overs were bowled from which only three runs were scored and it was 4 pm before the Players sent up the 100. At 4.48 pm, Richard was caught at mid-off for 64, out of 129 for seven. Those were the days when skill, whether in attack or defence, was fully appreciated. He hit only two fours and ran 29 singles in his first fifty of the season. The score finally scrambled to 192. On the third day, the Gentlemen, left 143 to win, scraped through by one wicket. Next, his county endured a horrendous match with Lancashire at Old Trafford. His scores, of 19 and 26, were the highest in each Notts innings – which totalled 68 and 67! However, the pitch was very bad –Selby was hit in the mouth and retired hurt.

In mid-June came a cameo of an exchange between Richard and Lord Harris when Notts met Kent at Canterbury. His Lordship, who was a fine batsman and the arbiter of English cricket for over fifty years, described their confrontation: 'There was an extremely fast UNDERHAND bowler, mostly along the ground, Crowhurst by name. He played for Kent *v* Notts and got a wicket or two, but he was no use against Richard Daft with his sure and graceful play. One ball hit Richard on the foot and hurt him considerably, and he turned to me in his most superior way, "This is not cricket, my Lord, this is not cricket."'

Notts returned south i-n mid-July, to play Middlesex on a perfect wicket. They amassed 368, which gave them a first-innings lead of 219. Richard batted with the utmost care until he had amassed 96, when he was lbw to C.K.Francis. He had batted for four hours, hitting one five and four fours. Middlesex followed on and were all out for 290, leaving Notts only 71 to win and with Richard contributing an undefeated 24, they won by nine wickets. He did not reach fifty again until the last match of the season, against Yorkshire at Sheffield in a drawn match. He had continued to compile useful scores, 20 and 44, in a defeat by Surrey at The Oval, 24 and 38 in an innings defeat by Gloucestershire at Trent Bridge, and eight and 34 there when Kent did not have to bat a second time to win the match.

At Cheltenham, Notts were trounced again. After Gloucestershire had hit up the moderate score of 235, the visitors twice collapsed against W.G. In the second innings, when they followed on, Richard held himself back for some reason, and while wicket after Notts wicket fell, so his wrath increased. At last he went in and as F.S.Ashley-Cooper put it, 'those who had been tempted (by W.G.) and fallen, watched his approach to the wicket with sympathy and no little interest.' Almost at once, Richard was out, caught Gilbert bowled W.G.Grace for 0, in W.G.'s famous square-leg trap: five Notts wickets fell at the same total and in 17 deliveries, W.G. took seven wickets without a run scored from his bowling, to finish with match figures of 17 for 89.

The final match of the season versus Yorkshire at Bramall Lane was ruined, with the first day totally washed out and the second day very miserable. Notts scored 110, Daft making six: Yorkshire replied with 145. Daft made 53 out of a second-innings total of 143 and Yorkshire batted out the final twenty overs, making 49 for one. Richard took his fiftieth first-class wicket during this match. The summer's results must have pained John Johnson, the former County Club secretary and a Nottingham solicitor for so long as he lived. His death occurred on 5 August, 1877. A very rich man, he was generous to Richard, leaving him £500, as well as £500 on trust to Richard Parr Daft, aged 13, whose godfather Johnson had been. He also left Richard all his cricket books, photographs and pictures.

Chapter Fourteen
Arrival of the Australians

Richard was destined to play the last seasons of his career in sub-standard English summers, 'unpleasant' to spectators and 'disgusting' to batsmen, in the words of '*Green Lilly*', but Shaw and Morley excelled in the damp conditions. So in 1878, Notts were back to their best with their great attacker, Alfred Shaw, returning like a giant refreshed. Morley captured 126 wickets at 9.92 each, while Shaw seized 92 for 11.70 runs each. Flowers and Barnes gave economical support.

In all, Notts took part in fourteen championship matches, a match against the Australians (the first of their tour) and two matches against the recently re-formed Leicestershire county club. These last two were not considered as first-class.

The Australians had embarked on a lengthy tour, starting with games in Australia, moving on to New Zealand, and sailing to San Francisco. After crossing the United States, they sailed from New York for Liverpool, where they landed on 13 May. By midday they were in Nottingham. An immense crowd of people had gathered at the railway station and the streets were lined by upwards of 8,000 spectators. Many of them expressed disappointment at the colour of the visitors, whom they evidently expected to find black. Within two hours of being toasted in champagne and hearing their captain, Dave Gregory, make the first of his many speeches on the tour, the Australians were practising at Trent Bridge.

The day of the game, 20 May, dawned bright and sunny but with dark clouds in the offing. T.P.Horan, a member of the eleven and later a well-known journalist, noted that the Notts side was strong and that it 'included Richard Daft, an experienced and great batsman on the verge of retiring from the game.' After the umpires had selected the strip for play, David Gregory won the toss for the visitors and chose to go in. The batting proved unmemorable and in 72.3 four-ball overs, the Australians were put out for only 63. At short slip, Richard neatly caught T.W.Garrett. After yet more rain, both Oscroft and Richard were dismissed with the score on ten, but by close of play, Notts were in much the better position, on 61 for four, with Selby and Wyld together.

The second day, Tuesday, was miserable and wet, but 10,000 spectators were present. At 11.30 am the rain came down and it seemed unlikely that there would be any play, yet at 1.30 pm they played. After a late lunch, Notts were 95 and no further wickets had fallen. The Notts total eventually reached 153 – a lead of 90. By close of play, the Australians were 44 for four wickets. Next day, there were only 400 on the ground as Shaw and Morley, who bowled unchanged during the match, finished off the visitors, who went down by an innings and 14 runs. A single-wicket match was staged to fill the rest of the third day.

The Australians' reception at Nottingham was far beyond their expectations. They were entertained at banquets twice during the match. Then, after visiting Nottingham Castle, admiring the town's parks and gardens, and observing the numbers of the rising generation practising cricket on the open space of the Forest, they were away in the train – Blackham, Midwinter, Murdoch, Spofforth and all – to London to their match with MCC and to immortality.

A week after the Australian match, Notts beat Lancashire by eight wickets in a game of low scoring. Richard stayed at the wicket for an hour for his 11 in the first innings. Then Notts returned, after an absence of thirty-eight years, to Town Malling in Kent, where they overwhelmed their hosts by an innings and 48 runs. Richard's 52 was the highest score in the match, and John Selby made 50. The home side could not match them, scraping 36 and 50, with Morley taking fifteen wickets.

Notts then played Leicestershire at Trent Bridge – the sides had not met since 1829. Notts won by ten wickets, Richard scoring 18. Derbyshire came to Trent Bridge nine days later. After the visitors put Notts out for 94, Derbyshire, in turn, collapsed for 55. Then Notts lost early wickets: Richard had been bowled for a duck in the first innings. In the second, he went in at number six and batted in his most assured form for about two and a half hours, hitting three fours and nine threes in his 69 not out. Derbyshire, left 216 to win, were bundled out by Alfred Shaw, leaving Notts winners by 122 runs.

Richard failed both times when Yorkshire demolished Notts at Bramall Lane, Sheffield, after amassing 419 in their only innings. He failed to recapture form as North and South, Derbyshire *v* the

All England Eleven, Gentlemen *v* Players, and the Notts match against Surrey all came and went.

The All England match at Derby is of historical and sentimental interest, as it was the last one played by the travelling Eleven. Richard showed his loyalty to the Eleven by this last appearance, and he still continued to give his connection with it pride of place in his business advertisements. It must be said, however, that the final All England Eleven consisted of nine Notts players, together with Richard Barlow and William McIntyre of Lancashire. Richard was bowled for two, in his only innings in a match which was won by England inside two days. North *v* South, the sides captained by Daft and Grace, was played at Trent Bridge as a belated benefit for George Parr, who went away with £250, 'a pecuniary result not as great as his old friends anticipated', according to *Wisden*. Then it was back to the front line. Richard journeyed to London for the fixture at Lord's for the Players beginning on 8 July, 1878. This match, which the Gentlemen won by 206 runs, saw a lot of good cricket, but not from him. The first six professional batsmen failed both times, but none fared so badly as Richard, with totals of one and nought. '*Green Lilly*' did not pull its punches: 'Richard Daft fielded badly, his sight is clearly going as he funked the ball. If he had not been playing, everyone would have complained: but evidently Richard is not himself.'

He failed, too, at Trent Bridge, contributing only two, but as Notts defeated Surrey it hardly mattered, and there were many failures, the highest individual score in the match was Shrewsbury's careful 27 not out. Surrey could make no more than 45 and 84 in their two innings and the only time runs came with any ease was when Oscroft and Shrewsbury knocked off the 42 needed for victory. He returned to Lord's for Bob Thoms' benefit match between Middlesex and Notts, who were set 271 for victory.

Richard joined William Oscroft with the score at 113 for two; his partner played a fine, free game until he was well caught for 77, when the score was on 151. Richard, who had made a useful 25 in the first innings, forced the pace in company with Wyld until at 6.20 pm he was caught at point for 40 at 224. The scoreboard showed that 47 runs were then needed as Alfred Shaw advanced to the wicket with only Morley to follow; with three minutes left a victory for Middlesex was still possible, but Shaw held on for a draw. *Lillywhite's Companion* was critical: 'The weather was beautiful and the ground like india-rubber, too quick for Daft in the field.'

Richard made 39 against Yorkshire at Trent Bridge when Notts avenged their innings defeat of a month before. They achieved the respectability of 228. Yorkshire, who batted only with ten men, were dismissed for 69 and followed on to be put out for 95. Morley and Shaw yet again bowled unchanged. Match after match that August was played on pitches spoiled by rain, and batsmen found run-getting very difficult. After a drawn game dominated by W.G. for Gloucestershire, Notts travelled to Clifton College for the return match beginning on 12 August. This was, astonishingly, Gloucestershire's first home match of the season: the weather was no better, the wicket was awful, and only 419 runs were made in the match. Unfortunately for Notts, Gloucestershire in their two innings scored 264 against their visitors' 155. Richard made three and nought, caught off W.G. second time around. He took a rest when Notts visited Derby and won an easy victory, but returned to the side when Middlesex came to Trent Bridge, and after Fred Morley had erased their first attempt for 85, Richard helped give Notts a good start, hitting up 30 out of 66 before being second out. Notts achieved a lead of 180: a blank second day and a drenching downfall on the last afternoon saved Middlesex from defeat. Richard did not travel to The Oval where Notts put out Surrey for 53 and 92 to win by 139 runs, but he presided over a one-sided match when Kent were dismissed for 94 first time around, and had struggled to 74 for 8 wickets in their second, amid showers which washed out the last part of the match.

In his batting for the county, Richard was no means prominent in the batting list in first-class matches, as can be seen from the table below:

	M	I	NO	R	HS	Ave	100	50
J.Selby	14	20	1	575	107	30.26	1	5
W.Oscroft	15	24	1	524	77	22.78	-	2
A.Shrewsbury	13	20	3	353	74*	20.76	-	2
R.Daft	12	17	1	331	69*	20.68	-	2
W.Barnes	15	23	7	307	56*	19.18	-	1
W.Flowers	15	22	2	372	57	18.60	-	2

On 3 September 1878, a major disaster struck when two river steamers came into collision on the Thames at Woolwich. One, the *Princess Alice*, was broken into two and, in horrible anticipation of the *Marchioness* incident 111 years later, over 700 people died.

The country was engulfed in a wave of shock and grief, and in a desire to help the bereaved, it was suggested that a match – The Australians *v* The Professionals of England – be played in London for the benefit of the relief fund. This was not entirely altruistic, as the two teams would take a share in the proceeds. This match did not take place, although the Australians did donate £100 to the fund. Eventually, on 19, 20 and 21 September, a game was arranged between those well-worn names, North *v* South, at The Oval, which realised £258 1s 6d for those in distress. The North, captained by Richard, who scored 13, won by an innings.

Chapter Fifteen
Eighteen Seventy Nine

In November, 1878, the Committee of MCC resolved: 'That no gentleman ought to make a profit by his services in the cricket field, and that for the future, no cricketer who takes more than his expenses in any match shall be qualified to play for the Gentlemen against the Players at Lord's.'

The description of the Australian tourists of 1878 on scorecards and in the newspapers as amateurs by the designation of 'Mr' or 'Esq' aggravated the grievances of the English professionals, which focused, of course, on W.G. *Lillywhite's Companion* for 1879 commented: 'The Note issued by MCC should have been published four or five seasons ago, but cricketers must be thankful that the leading club has, however late in the day, recognised an evil which has been injuring the best interests of the game for some years past.' It added: 'One well-known cricketer in particular has not been an absentee from the GENTLEMEN'S Eleven at Lord's for many years past, and that he has made larger profits by playing cricket than any professional ever made is an acknowledged fact.'

In fact, all three Graces were responsible for claiming unusually high match expenses. On 4 January, 1879 the journal *Bell's Life* published a letter from a member of the Gloucestershire County Cricket Committee. The topic? A claim for expenses submitted by E.M.Grace, as Hon. Secretary of the Gloucestershire Club, to the Surrey Club after the two sides met at The Oval. The total of £102 10s 0d was rejected by the Surrey authorities as being exorbitant. Each member of the Gloucester team claimed £4.10s 0d expenses, but in addition, W.G. claimed £15, Fred Grace £11, W.R.Gilbert £8, and E.M.Grace £20. Surrey cut the claim down to £80. *The Sportsman* paper commented that the amounts would have been excessive even for an exclusively professional team. W.G. expressed his deep regret and observed that he meant in future only to ask for his personal expenses.

But as W.G. was involved, nobody cared to take any action. There would never be anyone like him.

Another wet season gave little or no opportunity for Richard, or anyone else, to recover their form. For the tenth time, W.G. topped the first-class averages and he scored most runs, but his total was 880 at 35.20: no-one reached the thousand. Richard's figures in eleven first-class matches were 174 runs at 10.23, with a highest score of only 52. Notts had a prosperous season, losing only once and winning five out of their twelve county matches: almost all the unfinished games were in their favour. Lancashire, who had identical results, were linked with Notts by most authorities as joint champions, though *Wisden* placed Notts first.

Nottinghamshire's side of 1879 shared the title with Lancashire.
Standing (l to r): F.Morley, H.Holden (honorary secretary), R.Daft (captain),
W.Barnes, W.Oscroft, E.Browne (assistant secretary).
Seated: W.Flowers, A.Shrewsbury, A.Shaw, F.Wyld (wk), W.Wright, W.F.Story.
On the ground: J.Selby.

At Trent Bridge in July, Notts showed their bowling strength when, after scoring 159 in the first innings of the match, Shaw and Morley despatched Derbyshire in 86 balls for only sixteen runs. Often the art of Richard's captaincy lay in winding up his two great bowlers and leaving them on. When he did not travel to Canterbury at the beginning of June, William Oscroft led the side. After contributing a marvellous innings of 140 to Notts' total of 384, he saw Morley, Barnes and a newcomer, Walter Wright, bowl out Kent for only 126. When they followed on, he opened the bowling with Morley, and at the other end, to the general astonishment, put on Barnes, whose fast bowling did all that was required. Barnes' figures were seven wickets for 43 as Kent subsided for 78, leaving Notts a glorious victory by an innings and 180 runs. Clearly, the county had a replacement captain in waiting in Oscroft, who was by common consent the best professional batsman of the year. He scored 614 runs for Notts at 32.31. In the first-class batting averages, Oscroft finished fifth with 763 runs at an average of 26.31.

Richard began his season of 1879 with an innings of 41 against the strong Lancashire attack, putting on 83 for the first wicket with Oscroft, though the match petered out in a draw, with strong winds which made conditions extremely unpleasant. Richard Brown, a member of the Trent Bridge staff, was killed before the start of the match, falling off a ladder trying to untangle the flag from its pole, when the flagpole snapped. Alfred Shaw, in his sixteenth season in first-class cricket, celebrated his benefit with a match, North v South at Lord's, by taking six for 39 and eight for 21, but the occasion was not a happy one for Richard who, after the first day had been washed out, was easily caught at slip off W.G. with the very first ball that was bowled by him for only four in the second innings. The loss of the first day was ruinous for 'the emperor of bowlers', but W.G. generously asked for the proceeds of his own testimonial match to be given to Shaw. Individual subscriptions for W.G's testimonial had been coming in handsomely and in due course he received his presentation of £1,400 and a clock.

The figures show that, after Richard's 52 against Yorkshire in the second week of June, in nine innings he had a highest score of only 14. But figures may be deceptive. As to his 13 against MCC at Lord's, *Wisden* records that the wicket was 'awkward': the cricket was of great excellence as Richard and Oscroft faced good bowlers with their tails up for 80 minutes before, on changing ends, Rylott caught and bowled Richard when the total was 35. Notts then collapsed for 86 and lost by 16 runs. Again, three weeks later at the start of Gentlemen v Players, he batted carefully over an hour for 14, adding 39 with George Ulyett, who went on to make a truly valiant 61. At the end of the season, *'Green Lilly'* referred to 'Daft, whose wicket is still hard to get if the ground is true'. How seldom he had any assistance in that respect in his last few seasons!

In the first week of August, he was at Skegness appearing for the Notts Castle C.C. against Lincolnshire: bowled for two, he atoned with 50 in the second innings. This match was staged to open a new ground where Richard was part-proprietor. In mid-June, he had raised a Notts side to play Twenty-two of Wakefield and at the end of July his side took on MCC at Bestwood Park over two days, and immediately after that, Notts opposed an Eleven of Keighley. There is no indication that the county committee objected to this 'freelancing', but when Richard's relations as skipper of Notts with Captain Holden terminated at the end of 1880, the executive took a different view of this activity, with a disastrous effect on their relationship with their professionals.

Meanwhile, Richard had been raising a team to tour Canada and the United States. The final Notts fixture against Kent was brought forward by three days to enable them to depart for their voyage across the Atlantic. Any doubts about his own form were put aside amid the anticipation of his first overseas tour on which he embarked at the age of 43.

Chapter Sixteen
America

Over a period of twenty years, Richard had refused all offers to join overseas tours, even when he was asked to name his own price. His obligations to the business of the brewery at Radcliffe-on-Trent; to his 'Cricket, Football, Lawn Tennis and British Sports Warehouse' at 1 Lister Gate, Nottingham; and to his wife and family of five children had provided more than adequate reasons for his wintering at home. Now he followed the first overseas tourists from Britain who had ventured to Canada and the USA. His county career could not continue for much longer, and this could be his last chance to raise a strong side and a substantial sum from playing cricket and selling cricket paraphernalia. American cricketers on their side were anxious to receive further visitors: a letter published in *Bell's Life* on 1 February, 1879 was addressed to 'Teams Intending to Visit New York', inviting them to communicate with the President of St George's Cricket Club of New York. A member of the Nottingham Town Council, John Parr Ford, who was then in Philadelphia, made the arrangements for Daft's side and accompanied them on the tour. He had already acted as manager to George Parr's team in 1859. He was helped by Edwin Browne, who was Assistant Secretary of Notts C.C.C. from 1877 to 1894.

With such an experienced administration to back him up, Richard had little to do but run proceedings on the field and enjoy the novelty of the trip. The team was made up of professionals who were the *crème de la crème*, seven from Notts and five from Yorkshire. Richard, Arthur Shrewsbury, Alfred Shaw, William Oscroft, John Selby, Fred Morley and William Barnes were from Notts, accompanied by Yorkshiremen Ephraim Lockwood, George Ulyett, Billy Bates, Tom Emmett and George Pinder. They had arranged to play twelve matches, almost all against odds, in seven towns and cities in the eastern part of USA and Canada, between 9 September and 24 October.

On 28 August, the party lunched at the Angel Hotel in Liverpool before boarding the *S.S.Sardinian* and were in high spirits as she sailed down the Mersey on a remarkably fine evening. It did not last. In *Kings of Cricket*, Richard wrote: 'It was alright until we got out of the Mersey, which we did just before we sat down to dinner. I already began to feel queer, and directly the soup was placed in front of me I had to get up and make a rush for the door.' ... 'I got down to my berth and there I stayed until we ran into the St. Lawrence.' For others, the following morning brought brilliantly sunny weather as they gazed on the Giant's Causeway and the Isle of Arran. Once they were halfway across the Atlantic, the time passed pleasantly enough for the majority in a little exercise, conversation, reading, smoking and cards – mainly whist.

On 4 September, they saw their first iceberg, and in dense fog they entered the Gulf of St Lawrence, where for eight hours they were stranded. Eventually, they disembarked at Quebec but saw nothing of it as they were soon on the Grand Trunk Railway bound for Montreal and Toronto. There they found the city in a state of excitement as the Governor-General was visiting. The Marquis of Lorne, heir to the Duke of Argyll, was married to Princess Louise, the daughter of Queen Victoria and Prince Albert. There was no doubt that she and not the Duke was the focus of attention. Princess Louise was regarded as the most attractive and accomplished of the Queen's daughters. She was a sculptor and writer, and moved in much wider circles than other members of the Royal Family; her relationships with artists were the subject of gossip.

At Toronto, the Princess on the first day, and the Duke on the second, made visits to the cricket, and Richard was called from the field to be presented to each of them. He had a long conversation with the Princess. It must have been a memorable occasion for him – which is more that can be said for the cricket. Richard top-scored for the English team with 34, out of 101. Twenty-two of Canada did less well, scoring 31, but fared slightly better with 72 at their second attempt, leaving Shrewsbury and Bates only three to win. The pattern was repeated as the Englishmen played twice more at Toronto against Twenty-twos before moving on to Hamilton, Ontario, but the highest total of the opposition was no more than 76. The best individual effort was by a bowler named Logan, who had seven victims for 35 in the first match at Toronto and a further six wickets at Hamilton. Shrewsbury, 66, and Barnes, 59, had a big stand in the second Toronto match, and five tourists, including Richard, scored over 20 in Hamilton when they made 186, their highest score in Canada.

Would they meet a better class of opposition in the States? Eighteen of Detroit could manage only 59 in the opening fixture, which was spoiled on the third day by rain. At the end of September, 1879, they reached New York, where they faced Twenty-two of Central New York, whose 44 visits to the crease produced only 94 runs! On Staten Island the local club showed better form, scoring 67 and 94, and their professional George Lane, from Notts, took five for 57. A week later they travelled south to Philadelphia where Browne had some cause for enthusiasm, writing: 'It was a great satisfaction to find that we had in Philadelphia a first class set of cricketers with whom every exertion must be put forth and, not only that, there was a community where cricket was as popular as at Nottingham, Sheffield or Canterbury. At Germantown, a suburb of Philadelphia, there is a strong English colony at the hosiery and other factories. One day, during the three day match, we had nearly 12,000 spectators on the ground.' He noted: '700 or 800 ladies watched the game with the greatest interest ... they kept scoring sheets to keep an exact account of the game. The behaviour of the vast crowds was very orderly and though the working classes drink lager beer in considerable quantities, there was better behaviour than on an English ground.'

Against a Philadelphia fifteen, played on 10, 11 and 13 October, the Englishmen were put in to bat. Ulyett, accompanied by Oscroft, began brilliantly until he was caught behind. When Shrewsbury was run out, the score stood at 34 for three on a very fast, indeed fiery, pitch. Richard slaved away for an hour for no more than five runs. Oscroft and Bates made a long stand for the sixth wicket in contrasting styles – Bates (41) knocked the bowling all over the field, while Oscroft displayed patience and coolness for his 62. The touring side then made an enormous effort in the field and led by 79 on the first innings. They set Philadelphia 201 to win, and emerged as winners by 145 runs.

Richard's team stayed in or around Philadelphia nearly a fortnight, and Browne wrote enthusiastically about the city. There were fewer Irishmen there than he had observed in other American cities: except from the Irish, the side met with friendliness and courtesy. Yet, except for the bowling of Logan, the cricket of the opposition was poor. At the dinner for his side held after the Staten Island match, Richard, replying to the toast, observed that the cricket he had met in America had not been up to expectation: 'If they meant to improve, they must show more patience and play with a straight bat.' Browne had noted the play of the Twenty-twos at Toronto as 'a mere procession of batsmen . . . taking careful guard and surveying the weak places in the field, making a grand swipe at what they thought was the ball – then retiring looking foolish.' Yet, Richard and his side played each match with vigour and never deliberately threw a point away.

For more than half the tour there was not much financial reward: then, on 15 October, Richard's team played eighteen American baseball players at Brooklyn for the benefit of the English team, while the last match – Notts *v* Yorkshire – was played for the same cause. It was said that 25,000 attended the Brooklyn match, and this made the cricket financially successful for the tourists, while they also engaged in some useful merchandising. *Wisden* later reported that the tour had 'a satisfactory balance in hand.' While commerce was in the minds of several of the tourists, business back in England was probably engaging two of them, Shaw and Shrewsbury. They took the opportunity on tour to finalise their plans to set up a business that would rival Richard's. In 1880, they launched The Midland Cricket, Lawn Tennis, Football and General Athletic Sports Depot at 85 Carrington Street Bridge, Nottingham. In the 1881 edition of *Wisden Cricketer's Almanack*, Richard advertised his business two pages after the end of the editorial section: anyone opening the almanac at the front would find, opposite the title page, an advertisement for Shaw and Shrewsbury's own warehouse. Their business flourished under the canny and cautious Shrewsbury, who was still only 23 years old, and its early success may be regarded as the nail in the coffin of Richard's emporium.

The touring party returned to Liverpool on 3 November, 1879. There they were entertained at a banquet where the team presented Richard with a gold pencil case, to add to the books and curiosities that had been pressed upon him by admirers in the course of the tour. There was, too, a presentation to Alderman Ford and to Edwin Browne.

James Lillywhite's Cricketers' Annual ('Red Lilly'), in reporting on the tour, suggested that it had been as successful as any undertaken by English cricketers, adding that 'Daft's Twelve did much to raise English professionals in the estimation of sportsmen on the other side of the Atlantic. It was the fond hope and belief of the Twelve that their visit will have the effect of encouraging cricket in a marked degree. Baseball and lacrosse will no doubt still prove formidable rivals.' Over the winter of 1879/80, Richard and Edwin Browne made a tour of their own around Nottingham and its environs, giving lectures about their great adventure.

The trip had been successful for Richard, who had received requests from his hosts to recommend professional bowlers, and he advertised this agency facility in *Wisden* for 1880, stressing that clubs, colleges or schools who applied to him 'might rely upon his recommending those only who have satisfactory testimonials from their previous engagements, and who of his own personal knowledge are fitted for the post to which he recommends them.' Yet, even as he looked forward to this new element in his business and to the season of 1880, he must have learned of Shaw and Shrewsbury's decision to set up as his rivals. Later, he would learn from their advertisement in *Wisden* in 1881 that they were 'under the Patronage of the Marylebone Club'.

Meanwhile, he pressed on with another season of captaincy in what was to be one of the county's most brilliant summers ever.

Chapter Seventeen
Triumph and Tribulation

Wisden described Notts' record in 1880 as 'splendid': ten county matches were played, six won, three drawn, and only one lost. Their record 'entitled the county to the championship honours' of the year. Of the three drawn games, two were greatly in favour of Notts, while they wound up their season by defeating the Australians, a feat which no other side accomplished that year. They also defeated MCC by an innings. Notts had, indeed, an almost perfect side. The names of the team for the match against Lancashire at Trent Bridge included nine men who already had played or would play in Test Matches, which number did not include Richard, whose prime was past by the time international cricket started. The side comprised Oscroft, Scotton, Shrewsbury, Gunn, Selby, Barnes, Daft, Flowers, Shaw, Sherwin and Morley. It batted down to number nine, but the team's greatest strength still lay in the attack: Shaw and Fred Morley.

Apart from county games, the early part of the summer featured two matches between Daft's American Eleven and Eleven of England. In the first, played at Lord's in mid-May before a large crowd, the Eleven of England had all the best of the game. Richard made two and four, and England's more consistent first innings was good enough to bring them victory by 94 runs. Richard's men were much more themselves a fortnight later at The Oval, although rain had the biggest role in the proceedings. At the start, Richard played an innings of 38; only Billy Barnes with an aggressive 42 gave much support. In the second innings, Richard's side gave another mediocre performance, leaving their opponents only 106. In conditions all against good cricket, England slithered to 42 for five, with Humphrey out of the match, injured, so Richard's side had the best of it.

In the championship, Notts beat Lancashire and Middlesex twice and Yorkshire and Surrey once each. A feature of the season was the county's outstanding fielding: Sherwin at last established himself as wicket-keeper and this unquestionably helped sharpen up their performance, while '*Green Lilly*' commented that Richard's captaincy, too, was a good deal better than before.

Notts' own season did not begin until 3 June when they met Surrey at Trent Bridge. By the end of three days of heavy and frequent showers, Notts with eight wickets in hand required only 14 to win. Richard, opening the innings, was bowled for three. Alfred Shaw had ten wickets and Fred Morley seven. Surrey were left 85 to win, and Daft did not bat in the second innings, with rain interrupting play. Going on to Old Trafford, Notts easily beat Lancashire by five wickets. Fred Morley took nine wickets. Richard made 12, batting at eight, and was bowled for a single in the second innings.

Back at Trent Bridge ten days later, Notts beat Yorkshire by two wickets – Yorkshire 66 and 84, Notts 98 and 53 for eight. Richard's 25 was the highest score for his side. Shaw and Morley took all 18 Yorkshire wickets to fall to bowlers. Next, to Lord's for victory against Middlesex; Shaw and Morley bowled almost unchanged, with Morley capturing 12 for 81. Richard's score was one in Notts' first innings. Back at Trent Bridge, the sides' totals were Lancashire 72 and 46 and Notts 66 and 54 for six, resulting in a great win for Notts by four wickets. The only score exceeding 20 in the match was by Alec Watson, the Lancashire slow bowler, batting at ten, who hit 29. Richard scored nought and two not out, Alfred Shaw secured eight victims, and Fred Morley 10.

Ten days later, Notts were at The Oval. Play was delayed until nearly one o'clock on the first day, but at the close and in the wet, Notts, headed by Richard who batted finely for 47, were 208 for six: they climbed to 266 on the second day. Wind and a hot sun following on the rain of the previous day had caused the pitch to be in a very bad state when Surrey began their brief, but memorable innings.

Sensation followed. In the course of 39.2 four-ball overs, twenty-eight of them maidens, Morley and Shaw put Surrey out for 16. Shaw returned three for six and Morley seven for nine, with one extra, a leg bye. As '*Green Lilly*' put it, Notts were lucky to win the toss, and on paper the Surrey batting – five of them scored centuries for the county in their careers – was by no means weak. Surrey's total has remained the lowest innings total at this ground, one of course rather better known for high scoring. When the opposition played up more to form at their second attempt, Richard introduced Barnes and Flowers at exactly the right moment and they ran through Surrey's middle order, to leave Notts victorious by an innings and 65 runs. There followed a rain-interrupted draw against Gloucestershire at Trent Bridge.

On to 9 August, 1880 and Bramall Lane, Sheffield, in which Notts were defeated for the only time that summer. The weather was splendid and an immense throng of people assembled on each of the first two days: affected by the recent heavy rains, the wicket favoured the bowlers throughout. By the end of the first day, the scores read: Notts 102, Yorkshire 75 for nine. At the close of the next day, Notts, the second time around, had subsided for 92; the home side needed only ten more runs to win, which they soon obtained next morning.

In the return match between Gloucestershire and Notts at Cheltenham College, William Barnes took the opportunity to play a remarkable innings of 143. He entered with the score on two and was last out at 272. He hit eight fours, but W.G's cunning placement of the field resulted in his running as many as 47 singles. Richard was his only substantial supporter, compiling a steady 40 before he was splendidly caught by Fred Grace, who next day top-scored for Gloucestershire with 62. Two months later, only 30 years old, he was dead as the result of a chill. Notts had to chip away at their opponents' batsmen as it took 170.2 four-ball overs to grind them out for 172. As the home side's deficit was 100, they were compelled to follow on and it took Notts another 176.3 overs to dismiss them a second time: they were then only 71 runs ahead, but there was no more time for play.

Barnes played two further splendid innings when Middlesex visited Trent Bridge for the match beginning 19 August. Only two days were necessary as Shaw, Morley and Barnes bowled the visitors out for 93. Notts gained a lead on the first innings of 79; Middlesex next day slumped again before a late rally left Notts 73 for victory. They lost five wickets in gaining their objective. Richard stayed for a while with Barnes in the first innings and was in at the kill with an undefeated single. Notts finished the season as undoubted champions.

Much later, in September, came Notts' big match of the season. It was a great coup for Captain Holden to have arranged the fixture with the Australians. In the spring they faced a hostile cricket establishment after a fracas at Melbourne in the winter of 1878/79 when Lord Harris, captain of England, was assaulted on the pitch.

Only after their memorable match against the full strength of England at The Oval earlier that September of 1880, the first Test Match played on English soil – Barnes, Shaw and Morley were three Notts' players in that inaugural match – did they regain their popularity. They then found the counties, who had so recently scorned their requests for fixtures, anxious to make amends. So large crowds were expected at Trent Bridge. A high price had to be paid. The visitors' equivocal status, treating themselves as amateurs when they were here for the money, did not help either. However, their matches had drawn large crowds even though most of them were played against odds. As Peter Wynne-Thomas wrote: 'This ... match being an extra county game, Captain Holden wrote to the Notts players saying that the terms agreed between Richard and the tourists were that they take half the receipts and then, after expenses had been paid, the remainder be divided among the Notts eleven. In 1878, this arrangement had resulted in the tourists – amateurs, of course – being paid £19 each and the Notts players only £6. It was little wonder that Shaw and Shrewsbury and five other leading players told Captain Holden what he could do with his offer.' Three days before the match, they demanded £20 per man, and as the club was heavily committed to expenditure, the Captain had to agree. He got a little of his own back by paying £21 to the four Notts players who had not rebelled, but the club were to sustain a heavy loss on the match.

The contest was a wonderful climax to this season. The Australians had not been beaten by any county and there was wide interest in seeing how they would fare against the champions. Unfortunately, Spofforth, Bannerman and Slight were injured, so only ten of the touring party were available: they brought in Thompson from Melbourne as substitute fielder but batted only ten. Notts, after being 53 behind on the first innings, fought back and were set 131 to win. Arthur Shrewsbury and Barnes, coming together with the score at 9 for two, took the total to 97, at which Barnes was bowled for 42, leaving a target of 34, with seven wickets in hand. After Oscroft was out there ensued a succession of failures. Five men, including Richard, made only two runs between them. Two were still wanted when the last man went to the wicket and took guard in breathless silence: the silence was shattered as Alfred Shaw tipped his first ball over the slips for two. Shrewsbury was undefeated for 66, and was carried shoulder high in triumph to the pavilion.

The season's averages for county matches, given below, show the strengths of the Notts side, and the extent of Richard's decline, in spite of a few innings in time of need.

Batting and Fielding:

	M	I	NO	R	HS	Ave	100	50	Ct/St
W.Barnes	10	15	2	430	143	33.07	1	1	7
W.H.Scotton	10	15	1	252	63	18.00	-	2	5
A.Shrewsbury	10	17	3	206	33	14.71	-	-	11
J.Selby	8	12	0	172	32	14.33	-	-	8
W.Flowers	10	15	2	180	42	13.84	-	-	7
R.Daft	10	15	2	167	47	12.84	-	-	3
A.Shaw	10	12	5	86	30*	12.28	-	-	7
W.Gunn	10	17	4	141	29*	10.84	-	-	6
W.Oscroft	10	17	1	162	33	10.12	-	-	9
M.Sherwin	6	7	1	25	7*	5.00	-	-	7/3
F.Morley	10	11	1	42	19	4.20	-	-	10
F.Wyld	3	4	0	7	4	1.75	-	-	3/2

Played in one match: H.A.Cursham 4 (1 ct); W.Marriott 0; W.Wright 3.

Bowling:

	O	M	R	W	BB	Ave	5i	10m
A.Shaw	764.3	497	523	63	6-18	8.30	4	1
F.Morley	756.2	380	896	85	8-36	10.54	9	5
W.Flowers	192.1	92	223	20	4-17	11.15	-	-
W.Barnes	184.3	94	237	10	2-10	23.70	-	-

At the county's Annual General Meeting at the end of January 1881, the committee, with regret, announced his retirement. In his letter of resignation – he was now 46 – Richard wrote that he would be willing and anxious to assist the committee at any time. The committee's reaction was equally warm: 'The cordial thanks of all who are interested in county cricket are due to Richard Daft for the straightforward and honourable way in which he has at all times acted as captain of the county eleven, thereby setting an example worthy to be followed by all cricketers.'

There was a tendency amongst Richard's contemporaries to rank him among the good captains, rather than the great ones like V.E.Walker, A.N.Hornby or Lord Harris, and it is true that he was not often greatly tested as he always had at his command a very powerful professional combination. Because of his strong belief in his own capabilities and his high renown among cricketers, he seems, with rare exceptions, to have kept the Nottinghamshire team well in hand. His leading players all had long careers (except poor Summers), which suggests that they kept reasonably fit, and there were few indications, in public anyway, of disagreement in the ranks: chief among them were the Oscroft incident in May, 1875 and the spat between Tolley and W.G. in August, 1876. These were both on-the-pitch events, which were outside the control of the captain in the pavilion. This was emphatically not so in 1877 when Richard proved incapable of pulling the Gloucestershire game round in the face of Notts' collapse against the bowling of W.G.

On the field there are no indications that his bowlers ever refused to comply with his bowling changes, though William Oscroft implies that Richard's management was not always very imaginative. Of the match between Kent and Notts at Canterbury in 1879, Oscroft told *Old Ebor*: 'I got 140 in one innings – the highest individual score of that season in a county match. Kent had all their wickets to fall at lunch on the last day … it was just a question of getting Kent out before time. I was captain of Notts [Richard was preparing for his American tour], and Alfred Shaw and Morley were our principal bowlers. I went up to Shaw and said, "I think we'll start with Barnes. I don't think they can play him on this wicket." The result justified my anticipations, for we got them all out by about 5 o'clock and won easily. Barnes' analysis was 29 overs, 9 maidens, 43 runs, 7 wickets. After the match, Lord Harris came up to me and said, "Oscroft, what induced you to put Barnes on instead of Shaw after lunch?" I replied, "Why, my Lord? I felt sure that you couldn't play him so well as Shaw on this wicket." … His Lordship answered, "You were quite right … but you must bear in mind there isn't another captain in England who would have substituted for Alfred Shaw at the commencement of an innings."'

The other counties, save Yorkshire led by Tom Emmett, were all captained by amateurs, but few examples of rank-pulling over Richard have come to light. The MCC match at Lord's in 1870 contained some anomalies in addition to the injury to Summers, but apart from the odd skirmish with Harris, Richard does seem to have held his own: and he was able to point to the fine record of the Nottinghamshire eleven under his captaincy. Notts played 104 matches in the ten seasons of Daft's captaincy from 1871 to 1880. He played in the side in 95 of them, captaining it in all the matches in which he played. Notts won 47 of those matches, lost 21 and drew 27.

In Richard's time, the title of champion was awarded by the press as a matter of judgement, rather than through any 'official' operation of a scheme of points. In some years, there was no consensus as to which country was entitled to the crown. These days *Wisden* says 'the title of champion county is unreliable before 1890.' However, it then lists Notts as 'the most generally selected' champions in 1871, 1872, 1873 (shared with Gloucestershire), 1875, 1879 (shared with Lancashire) and 1880. This remarkable record demonstrates what a fine team the county had built up over 15 years or so.

If we accept that Richard led Notts in six successful championship campaigns, then we can compare him to Lord Hawke, whose Yorkshire side won the competition eight times, and to John Shuter of Surrey and Brian Sellers of Yorkshire, both six. He stands ahead of Stuart Surridge who led Surrey to five championships and two more recent and formidable practitioners of the art, Brian Close and Mike Brearley, whose sides won it four times. Cricket has no doubt become more complicated since our subject's time, but he still had to decide on strategy and tactics, motivate players, decide batting orders, change bowlers and set fields better than opposing captains. There can be little doubt that he did all those things well by the standards of his period.

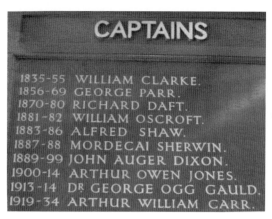

Daft and five other professional Nottinghamshire captains are listed on this honours board at Trent Bridge.

Richard was duly elected on to the committee and so was involved in one of the most unhappy situations which the county ever experienced, a situation to which he had unwittingly contributed. Reverting to amateur status, he played only twice for Notts in 1881. At the beginning of June, he journeyed to Old Trafford where the home side gave Notts a ten-wicket defeat. Richard made five and seven. It was eight weeks before he turned out again, this time at Trent Bridge, against his favourite foes, Gloucestershire. He fell lbw to W.G. for one. Gloucestershire had to follow on. W.G. had a lesson to teach his opponents and the sequel must have been hard labour for Richard and his colleagues as W.G. dominated bowlers and fieldsmen on his way to 182, which was the highest individual score up to that date in a county match at Trent Bridge, while the Gloucestershire score climbed to 483 and Notts' first-innings advantage was forgotten.

In the Lancashire match, Notts had introduced no fewer than seven replacements for absent members of their side: only the youthful William Gunn, William Oscroft, Richard's successor as captain, Mordecai Sherwin and Richard remained from the eleven of 1880. There had been a profound dispute between Captain Holden and the Notts committee on the one hand and Arthur Shrewsbury, Alfred Shaw and five other prominent players, Barnes, Flowers, Morley, Selby and Scotton, on the other. The cause arose after the Bradford cricket authorities had asked Shaw and Shrewsbury to take a Notts side to play a Yorkshire eleven at Horton Park Avenue, Bradford. The two Notts professionals had inaugurated the ground the previous year with a match between their side and the Australians. In 1881, however, things were not the same – Captain Holden objected to their proposed match, only to be told (what he already knew) that Richard had organised a similar match without objection from the Notts executive. The entrepreneurial duo might have added that Richard had raised sides including Notts players on at least four earlier recorded occasions in recent years.

Richard's warm relationship with Holden had guaranteed acquiescence in these matches, but with his retirement, Holden, a domineering personality at the best of times, took a totally contrary line with Shrewsbury and Shaw. They played for the county in the annual Colts' match, but stalemate ensued when, following Holden's rejection of their request, the two in turn refused to meet him. Holden thought that he would exact revenge by sending new forms of contract to the principal Notts professionals. They realised that if they signed up they would be committed to play 12 three-day matches for the county to the exclusion of other paid employment, but the county committee would be under no obligation to select them.

All seven regular players were included in the team for the opening fixture against Sussex at Trent Bridge on 26 and 27 May – only two days were needed as Notts won by an innings. Then the committee agreed to engage five of the seven, Shaw and Shrewsbury together with Morley, Selby and Barnes, but not Scotton or Flowers: the players held together and withdrew their labour, so a week later when Notts played Lancashire, all seven were left out of the side and Richard came in. From then on the executive produced a succession of ad hoc sides, called by some 'Holden's Marionettes'. In early August, Wilfred Flowers rejoined the eleven for the match against Gloucestershire at Clifton, and made a powerful point in his own favour by taking 12 wickets for 85 runs. Subsequently, Selby and Barnes and then Morley returned to the fold before the end of the season of 1881, but Shaw and Shrewsbury did not return until the following spring. The improvised outfit won four matches, which included the defeat of Surrey at Trent Bridge and – wonderfully – of Gloucestershire at Clifton.

Lillywhite's Cricketers' Annual of 1882 summed up the unhappy episode: 'The governing body had acted very unwisely in Daft's case and established a precedent which proved very inconvenient. The only indictment was one of inconsistency ... '

The Notts dispute was made up by the next season, and the county's cricket entered another period of prosperity, but 1881 must have been embarrassing for Richard. Newly elected to that Valhalla, the Notts Committee, he saw his side disintegrate in circumstances regarded by the majority of critics as highly prejudicial to his former colleagues, and found himself among their opposition, while the cause of the dispute was said to be a bad precedent arising from the Executive's collusion with him!

Meanwhile, Shaw and Shrewsbury had leisure to promote their business. Shrewsbury, intelligent, cool and a bit finicky, was the brains behind the new set-up and he lost no time in acquiring premises and advertising the business. The attitude of the partnership was a purely commercial one: any damage to Richard's finances would be a matter for Richard. In his publicity, Shrewsbury coolly described himself as a 'Member of American Team, 1879' – Daft's team.

Meanwhile, Richard found his energies heavily engaged. *Scores and Biographies* gives particulars: 'In 1881, he became mine host of the hotel on the Trent Bridge Ground, and with his brewery at Radcliffe-on-Trent and his cricket and athletic emporium in St. Peter's Square [*sic*] in Nottingham, his hands were pretty full.'

Daft's businesses advertised in a local directory in 1881.

Chapter Eighteen
Many Preoccupations

Towards the end of his career, Richard's portrait was painted by Frank Miles, one of the sons of the Rector of Bingham. A brother was R.Fenton Miles, who had played for Gloucestershire as a slow left-arm bowler in the 1870s, under the captaincy of W.G. In *Kings of Cricket,* Richard remembered: 'The hours I spent in Miles' studio were amongst the pleasantest of my life. To him I related many of the stories which appear in these reminiscences and he, in his turn, related some most amusing anecdotes. I sat to him, I think, on about forty occasions, but I am bound to state that the sittings were not of long duration, for we always finished off with several games of tennis.' Miles had studied on the continent, exhibited at the Royal Academy, and became well-known as a genre, portrait and marine painter. His best-known portrait was of Mrs Lillie Langtry. However, all was not sweetness and light. He shared a house for a time with Oscar Wilde until his father heard of rumours about Oscar and insisted that they part. Following this enforced separation, by 1891 Miles had 'lost his wits' and he ended his days in Brislington Asylum, Bristol.

Frank Miles' portrait of Richard Daft now oversees proceedings in the Trent Bridge pavilion.

In 1880, Richard's young brother-in-law, Butler Parr junior, came of age and was entitled to his half-share of his father's estate, which included the brewery at Radcliffe. Instead of becoming a partner in a small local brewery, young Parr joined the Home Brewery Company, of which he eventually rose to be chairman, and was associated in other undertakings controlled by the famous industrialist, Sir John Robinson of Newark. Meanwhile, he wanted his share of his father's assets: the brewery was sold by auction, which took place at the beginning of July 1880. It was sold to Richard for £4,050, the equivalent of £240,000 today. At a price, he was now his own man and not just the brewery agent, although there was still a rival brewery in Radcliffe. Richard had now been in business at Lister Gate for fourteen years. Later in the decade, he moved his British Sports Warehouse to St. Peter's Square, Nottingham, where there was an immense stock for every sport. By the following year, he had added portmanteaus, bags and cases for the increasing band of holiday-makers. Around 1881, Richard became licensee of the Cliff Inn at Radcliffe for a ten year term, although a Mr Bampton may have run the pub for him. He also had an interest in the Chesterfield Arms at Bingham, as well as the Trent Bridge Inn.

The loan which Richard had to raise was a great handicap to him in the years to come, and the eventual decline in his business career was at least partly due to the resulting high payments of interest. Another reason, surmises Peter Wynne-Thomas, was Richard's lack of attention to his emporium: a third was the increasing competition in Nottingham after not only Shaw and Shrewsbury, but also William Gunn, opened rival businesses. Gunn set up on his own in 1885 at 14 Carrington Street, Nottingham – midway between Richard's premises and those of Shaw and Shrewsbury. Gunn had, as noted, worked originally for Richard. Thomas Moore, who left Richard's business where

Richard Daft, as a confident businessman, in the 1880s.

107

he had been manager for eleven years, joined Gunn and became his partner.

Richard was an active participant in the village life of Radcliffe. When the Radcliffe Conservative Association was formed in 1880, he was an early member and was among the notables who attended the first dinner in November, 1881. A less civilised event was a meeting held by the Liberals in October, 1885, which was disrupted beyond recall by a posse of their opponents who were egged on by three members of the Daft family which, according to the report, included Richard himself. The other two were presumably Richard the younger, then aged 21, and Harry, aged 19. When the Liberals renewed their meeting some weeks later, the speaker remarked: 'I would have thought that in Radcliffe, Parr and Daft would have known how to receive one of the opposite team.' By 1886, Richard was a member of the Conservative committee.

For a period in the 1880s, he served on the Board of Guardians, who were responsible for the administration of the Poor Law, and was elected a member of the Finance Committee, but by 1887 he was finding it difficult to get to their meetings. He was also a sidesman at the parish church.

His political views indirectly brought him before a session of the Revision Courts, held in September 1885, and concerned with municipal voting rights. The Liberals objected to his having a vote by virtue of his occupation of the refreshment booths on the Trent Bridge ground. They argued that as Richard let the booths, the persons who sold the drinks were the true occupiers. After hearing from the Secretary of the County Cricket Club that Richard paid the rates and that the booths had been erected at Richard's expense, the objections were dismissed and he retained his (Tory) vote.

In 1881, he was the first professional cricketer ever to be elected to the Notts committee. Apart from Robert Tolley and, until 1872, his father-in-law, Butler Parr, he was the only cricketer of distinction to belong to that body. Richard's experience was never again as uncongenial as it had been in 1881. On the field, Notts went from strength to strength, especially after Alfred Shaw replaced the ailing William Oscroft as captain in 1883. After sharing the title with Lancashire in the previous year, they headed the championship table in 1883, losing only two matches over the period 1883 to 1886. In 1885, Richard stood down by rotation in accordance with club rules, but he returned the following year and stayed on the committee until 1889.

Richard's son Harry played 190 first-class matches for Notts from 1885 to 1899 and umpired 42 Oxford University matches from 1900 to 1914.

Harry Daft first appeared in the Notts team in 1885. He was a wonderfully promising young player who had played his first match in the Eleven at Trent College at the age of only 12 and kept his place for four years. He was just 17 when he hit his first century in club cricket in 1883, hit over 1,200 runs the following summer, and just a year later enjoyed his first trial for Notts when he played for the county against MCC at Lord's. With totals of 23 and 10 not out, he was the most successful of the county's batsmen. Scores of 52 for Notts against England and 40 against Gloucestershire followed, and with one break he remained a regular in the county side until 1898. Yet his batting at that level never progressed beyond determined defence, and he certainly never rivalled his father. In club cricket, he was a prolific scorer and he, Richard and Richard junior hit up 47 centuries between them over the period 1885 to 1897.

Harry earned greater fame in the world of Association Football, as a member of Notts County A.F.C. From 1888, he captained the team, for which he made 137 League appearances and was capped five times for England.[2] His brother, Richard Parr Daft, played only once in first-class cricket, in 1886 – he scored 5 against Surrey at Trent Bridge – and ten years later made three appearances for Berkshire in the Minor Counties championship. His abilities lay in a different direction as he helped Richard put together his reminiscences *Kings of Cricket* and later performed the same task

---

2   He captained the England side against Ireland in Belfast in March, 1892, scoring both his side's goals.

for William Caffyn's *Seventy-one Not Out*. He was a prolific run-maker in club cricket, but it was said that he had no liking for the first-class game.

In *Kings of Cricket*, Richard says that he was fully determined not to give up the game 'for no-one knew better than myself the great benefit which is to be derived from it as regards health.' At the age of 45 he played in as many club and local matches as he would have done if he had been quarter of a century younger. Richard claimed to have amassed 17 centuries after completing his fiftieth year. He always enjoyed a fixture against the North Riding of Yorkshire and with good reason: in 1886, when 50 years of age, he hit up the highest score of his career, 222. In a match against them at Middlesborough in 1887, he contributed 115 to the total of 462 amassed by an Eleven of Notts: young Richard outscored him with 124. Harry's total was 67 not out in the second innings, and brother-in-law Butler Parr also played well for 43. Richard also captured five wickets in North Riding's first innings. In 1889 at Osberton Hall, Nottingham, against Wincobank, he returned an even better analysis of nine wickets for 23.

Another favourite venue for Richard was Skegness on the Lincolnshire coast, already known as a trippers' paradise. In August 1882, the Daft family took on The Town at cricket. The home side collapsed for 72 as Richard claimed seven wickets: then, going in second wicket down, he hit an unbeaten innings of 103, out of the family's total of 144. Only Charles Daft's son, C.F. junior, of the others scored double figures.

Richard's links with Skegness went back to 1879 when the *Nottingham Journal* reported that he was one of the proprietors of the new ground. In 1886, the Australian tourists were persuaded to play Sixteen of Skegness and District. It was the only match the team played against odds. The wicket was described as fast and true, but this did not help the visitors, who were bowled out for 103 and 148. The sixteen (fourteen of whom had played first-class cricket) led by 78 runs on the first innings, and lost only six wickets in achieving victory when Richard made the winning hit just before time on the third day. Photographs still hang in the pavilion as mementos of the occasion. It was 65 years before another Australian Eleven returned to Skegness to avenge that defeat by an overwhelming margin. All the participants then were women.

Throughout the 1880s, he kept up his form. He did not reach three figures in 1881, that year of adjustment, but in 1882, in addition to his century for the Daft XI at Skegness, he hit up 105 for Nottingham Commercial versus Newark: 1883 brought two large innings, 154 not out for Nottingham Commercial against the Leicester Town Club in mid-June, and 178 for his own Eleven versus Trent College – which both his sons attended. That season, Richard also made a brief return to first-class company when he played in two matches in the Scarborough festival, including one for MCC. It was very unusual for a former professional cricketer to turn out for MCC as an amateur in a first-class match: he scored two and 23. 1884 was the first year in which Richard and both his sons, R.P., aged 20, and Harry, aged 18, all reached three figures.

In 1886, when he was 50, in addition to his 222 at Scarborough, he hit 138 for Skegness versus Alvaston, whose attack included a name from long before – John Platts. In 1887 came his 115 at Middlesborough against the North Riding of Yorkshire: the following year his fine batting in the same fixture produced an innings of 89. In 1889, he had an average of 41 for 25 innings. He exceeded even this form in 1891, hitting a century early on and following this with two more hundreds before reaching three figures again in the last week of July at Trent Bridge against opposition of real quality, including the Hon Alfred Lyttleton, the Test player. That summer, Richard hit four other scores of 50 or more, and a further five which exceeded 40.

Chapter Nineteen
A Match Too Far?

At the end of July 1891, Arthur Shrewsbury hurt his hand and was unavailable for Notts' needle match against Surrey beginning on the August Bank Holiday. The Notts Committee were well aware of Richard's continuing prowess on the cricket field: they asked him to play at The Oval, and without hesitation he accepted. This was a risky undertaking: Surrey were all-powerful. The mainstays of their bowling were George Lohmann, with his variations in pace and style – 'neither fast nor slow man'; Bill Lockwood of great pace with a well-concealed slow delivery; and John Sharpe, very quick left-arm. All of them were England cricketers, contributing to a formidable attack: Lockwood and Sharpe were both Notts-born. That year, Surrey won 12 of their 16 matches. Many critics felt that it was a weakness on the part of the Notts committee to have to call upon a man in his fifty-sixth year to fill a vacancy in an emergency. Richard, though, felt in fine fettle: he had scored 107 the day before journeying up to London on the Sunday which preceded the Bank Holiday. 'For some reason or other I never felt more fit for run-getting since I first began to play' was his happy recollection. He had made his first-class debut at The Oval thirty-three years before: on this occasion, with the weather threatening storms, Surrey won the toss and elected to bat, and so Richard stepped out once more on the turf and took up his position at point. He had never fielded there in his professional career. 'Although I tried my utmost to keep my attention on the game, my thoughts would constantly stray away of themselves to memories of other days. I thought of the match in 1858 and of those who took part in it, and tried to reckon up how many were now alive of the two old elevens and how many had been bowled out by the great bowler, Death.'

The Times reporter noted: 'It is a curious thing that he should have come back after a lapse of ten years and then as a substitute for Shrewsbury who has imitated him in style with a success that made the copy *almost equal to the original.* Sunday's storms had left the ground terribly soft. Showers prevented the turf growing as treacherous as it would without rain. The weather was bright, but, though of brief duration, the showers were heavy.'

In front of a crowd estimated at 25,000 on the Bank Holiday, Surrey accumulated a total of 176. The scene is set out for us by *Leather Hunter*, A.J.Gaston of Brighton, whose piece in the periodical *Fores's Sporting Notes* gave Richard particular pleasure. He suggested that there was a treat at The Oval such as they never hoped for again. 'Richard Daft was to figure in a first-class match once more! – in fact the match of the season – for neither Gentlemen versus Players, nor North versus South, excites the interest that Nottingham versus the premier county does; nevertheless, The Oval would certainly not have drawn twenty-five thousand together but for the presence of the veteran in the Midland team. What was our surprise when on Mr. Shuter's putting Nottinghamshire in the field, our old friend was placed at point. The surprise grew more intense as we watch the neatness and smartness with which he answered each appeal of the batsmen. The wicket playing extremely dead ... there was not the solitary chance of a catch, but many a run was saved by the wonderful power the veteran showed in "getting down to them."' Alas, *Leather Hunter* was unable to describe Richard's innings, which did not start until the following day when there were 10,000 present; Richard himself wrote in *Kings of Cricket*: 'On my leaving the pavilion for the wickets, I received such an outburst of applause as perhaps neither I nor any other cricketer ever experienced before. Much as I have valued all the hearty receptions I have received and the kind things that have been written of me during my long career, yet I declare solemnly I never felt such a thrill of gratitude as when I heard that mighty shout ascend from the vast multitude assembled on that time honoured enclosure, and for some minutes I was deeply affected. If I had been accorded this welcome at home, I should not have felt it so much, but to be received in this manner on the ground where I played my first great match was indeed affecting.'

The morning was bright and hopeful, and play started with the Notts score at 34 for two. With 20 added, Lohmann bowled Barnes, who was succeeded by Richard; he immediately went on the attack, three times driving Lohmann for two. With 10 more added, Gunn was caught at mid-on. Notts' best chance of making a good response was gone – 64 for four. Joined by Attewell, Richard drove Lohmann to the off for four and to the on for two. *The Times* man reported that he exhibited all his old prettiness of style and coolness. Lockwood then bowled Attewell – 70 for five; and C.W. Wright first ball – 70 for six. These disasters were followed by an outbreak of hail – a pity that it had not poured down ten minutes earlier – followed by steady rain, causing the match to be abandoned for the day. It was 5 o'clock and Notts still needed 27 runs to save them from the follow-on. They did not get them. On the third morning, Lohmann had Richard caught low down at slip and that was the end of Notts' resistance. At the second attempt, Richard opened the innings with Flowers, but the latter was almost at once caught at cover-point. William Gunn joined Richard and they survived together for 17 minutes, adding five singles, before Gunn was bowled. Barnes, in turn, stayed with Richard for 35 minutes more: then Richard, sensing the futility of the exercise, lashed out and was caught in the deep, and who could blame him? He had placed two runs to his credit out of seven in just under an hour. That he, Gunn and Barnes had made such heavy weather of facing Lohmann and Lockwood was small encouragement to their colleagues: the two Surrey bowlers were unchanged during the Notts innings of 44.

The papers seized upon the point that the Dafts, father and son, had played together in a first-class match, but this was not unique. For example, back in 1851, William Lillywhite and his sons James and John had played for Surrey against Middlesex at The Oval and they repeated the feat at Lord's two years later. William Clarke and his son Alfred played in the same elevens in nine matches for Notts in the 1850s. Richard and Harry were twice more to repeat *their* double act.

Richard had shown that he retained his powers of defence, and he was encouraged to turn out twice more. A fortnight or so later, he journeyed to Clifton where his reunion with W.G. was sadly spoiled by rain. Arthur Shrewsbury, fit again, played a magnificent innings of 94: he scored his runs in 2½ hours before being sixth out. Richard joined him at 59 for three, and shared in a stand of 29 before being finely caught down the leg-side by Jack Board, the keeper, from the bowling of – who else? – W.G. Notts completed their innings at 205 on the first day. There was no play on the second, and the home side struggled to 73 for five on the third, in a couple of hours before the match was given up.

Richard returned to Trent Bridge for Notts' last match against Middlesex. This game, too, was ruined by the rain: there was no play on the first day and only 1½ hours on the second. The last day's play saw Notts blown away for 84. Both Richard, playing as an amateur, and Harry, a professional, were bowled for ducks by J.T. Hearne, whose figures were nine for 32. Middlesex fared little better, scoring 97. William Attewell had six wickets for 35. So finally terminated Richard's first-class career.[3]

Nottinghamshire's side in 1891, which finished fourth of nine in the championship.
Standing (l to r): H.Coxon (scorer) W.Gunn, W.Barnes and W.Flowers. Seated: F.Shacklock, C.W.Wright, J.A.Dixon (captain), R.Daft, Wm.Attewell and M.Sherwin (wk).
On the ground: R.Bagguley and H.B.Daft.

This same summer, on 23 June, 1891, George Parr died. Richard was a mourner at his funeral and later wrote a tribute to Parr 'who was buried with a branch of the tree at Trent Bridge, known as George Parr's tree, in his grave, the trunk of which has received many a hard knock from the ever memorable and unequalled leg hits of this magnificent batsman.'

---

3   Richard was 55 years 300 days on the third day of this match. Only three older players have appeared in the 'official' championship. These are Rev R.H.Moss (Worcestershire) who was 57 years 91 days when he played against Gloucestershire at New Road in 1925: W.G.Quaife played for Warwickshire in 1928 and C.E.de Trafford for Leicestershire in 1920, both at the age of 56.

Richard continued his cricket for another six years or so; one of his innings remains as a proud testament to his fitness and dedication. On 15 and 16 August 1893, Skegness and District scored 79, to which South Notts replied with 328. Skegness batted a second time scoring 44 for four, leaving the match drawn. The visitors' scorecard read as follows:

1	W.Whitlock	b Woodley	15
2	A.Phillips	c and b Carter	4
3	A.Oliver	b Woodley	1
4	H.B.Daft	c and b Lovett	27
5	R.Daft	c Disbrowe b Carter	144
6	R.P.Daft	c Disbrowe b Lee	80
7	A.L.Checkland	b Booth	0
8	C.Hassall	b Booth	6
9	J.Francklin	not out	38
10	J.L.Checkland	b Carter	0
11	W.Mee	b Booth	6
	Extras		7
	Total		328

This was a remarkable feat of endurance for a veteran in his fifty-eighth year. How did he maintain his condition and form? At his home, The Rosery, he kept an asphalt tennis court which he also used for cricket practice: he had his own skittle alley, too. Every day he made a point of walking at least two miles and, taking to tennis quite late in life, played the game enthusiastically all year round: and he never failed to take his cold bath in the morning. He hunted, shot, fished, played lacrosse, to which he was an early devotee, and he cycled and skated, too.

He hardly practised cricket between matches, though he always made a great point of having a few balls before the start of a game. He ends the section 'Hints on Cricket' in his book *Kings of Cricket*: 'Many people used to think that my wrist play was the best part of [my batting] and [this] . . . has, in my opinion, been owing to the great use I have made of the dumb-bells - fairly heavy ones - I use every morning of my life.'

Chapter Twenty
Kings of Cricket

J.A.H.Catton, the sports journalist, claimed to have been the first to suggest that Richard should write his reminiscences, and stressed that he would make every effort to place the manuscript if he persevered with it. With the material help of Richard junior, Richard did persevere; the result was *Kings of Cricket.* Catton sold the manuscript to Tillotson and Son of Bolton for £325, of which the present-day equivalent is about £17,000. Tillotsons offered the memoirs for serial publication in *The Athletic News*, published by Hultons in Manchester.

In the autumn of 1891, Richard was in touch with the distinguished man of letters, Andrew Lang, who replied to him on 27 October:

> I shall be pleased to see your manuscript, but till I see it I cannot say, of course, whether my assistance would be of any advantage to it. It may be better without me. Probably, the best plan would be for you to have it typewritten; in that form it is easily read and corrections can easily and inexpensively be made. Corrections on proof sheets are expensive.
>
> ... If the ms. were typewritten, I could easily see whether my assistance would be of any use or not. Till I see it, of course, it is impossible to decide.
>
> faithfully yours
Andrew Lang

> You have probably played against my brother, T.W.Lang, who used to bowl for Gloucestershire.

It was a great feather in Richard's cap that he attracted Lang's interest, as he was one of the great literary figures of his time. *The Dictionary of National Biography* describes Lang as scholar, folklorist, poet, and man of letters. He was a Scot, born at Selkirk on 31 March 1844, and he must have been, of all his race, among the keenest on the history and practice of the game of cricket. He is best remembered for his collections of fairy stories:

> Books yellow, red and green and blue
> All true or just as good as true.

Lang went on to write, as an introduction to Richard's book, one of the most famous essays on cricket, which has been anthologised over and over again, and was actually republished on its own in 1992 to mark the centenary of the publication of the work it was written to introduce.

By the end of November 1891, the matter, if not the manuscript, was in the hands of Tillotson and Son. Tillotsons offered J.W.Arrowsmith, the Bristol-based publisher and printer, the volume rights, including that introductory chapter from the pen of Andrew Lang and the use of at least 50 photographs and pictures.

Arrowsmith, an entrepreneurial and provocative man to do business with, sought further particulars: Tillotsons complied before offering him the entire British and American volume rights for the sum of £200. Arrowsmith accepted by return, although the date of delivery of the typed manuscript hung in the air. Tillotsons

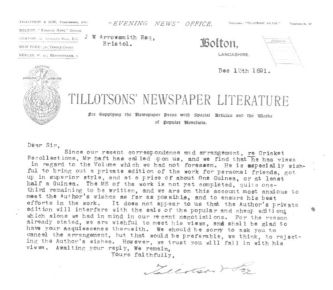

Part of the correspondence between agent and publisher about Daft's book, 'Kings of Cricket'.

wrote on 12 December, 1891 that Richard was 'especially wishful to bring out a private edition for personal friends, got up in superior style and at a price of about one guinea or, at least, half a guinea.' The book was to be publicised in the magazine *Cricket*; and Richard told a correspondent that it would be serialised in the newspapers from about the end of April and would run on to September, 1892. He continued: 'When it comes out in book form it will contain between 70 and 80 illustrations. You might say that it contains my experiences from quite a boy until the present day. Giving an account of all the great players I have met during that time and other celebrities in different walks of life . . . together with a great stock of anecdotes. An account of the development of cricket during the last fifty years and hints of [*sic*] the game, with engravings illustrating all the positions and hits almost that a batsmen can make."

In addition to the well-known photographers, Hawkins of Brighton, two long-established collectors, Charles Pratt Green of Malvern and Thomas Padwick of Redhill, supplied pictures. The development of reproduction had reached the stage where the volume could be quite inexpensively filled with illustrations in photogravure.

On 29 February 1892, *Athletic News and Cyclists' Journal* reported: 'The proprietors of *Athletic News* have pleasure in announcing that they have arranged to publish a new work on our national pastime by Richard Daft, who has played in first-class cricket since 1858. It will be entitled *The King of Cricket*.' The mere suggestion of that title must have been enough to bring a change of mind; either it would have brought a charge of arrogance against the author, or misled readers into thinking that the book was by, or about, W.G. Grace. When the first instalment did appear on Monday, 11 April, the title was changed to *Kings of Cricket*, and so it remained as instalment succeeded instalment until, on 15 August, *Athletic News* carried an article 'Cricket' by Andrew Lang, which was to form the Introduction.

Kings of Cricket, subtitled 'Reminiscences and Anecdotes with hints on the game' appeared in two editions. One was published by Simpkin and Marshall, London and Arrowsmith, Bristol in 1893: the other in a subscribers' limited edition by Tillotson and Son. But how limited? The generally accepted number is 150 copies, but there are indications that that number was greatly exceeded. In February 2003, John McKenzie's catalogue contained a copy of the

RADCLIFFE ON TRENT,
near NOTTINGHAM.

My dear Sir

I enclose the photograph as promised. Many thanks for your kindly promising to ... a paragraph to cricket. The work will, I expect commence to run through the newspapers about the end of April and will continue to do so until about the middle or end of Septr. When it comes out in book form it will contain between 70 & 80 illustrations. You might say that it contains my experiences from ... a boy until the present day. Giving an account of all the great players I have met during that time & other celebrities in different walks of life to that of cricket. together with a great stock of anecdotes. An account of the development of cricket during the past fifty years; & hints of the game ... with engravings illustrating all the positions & hits almost that a batsman can make. Both the Hints on the Game & the work generally will contain many more illustrations than any work published hitherto connected with the national game. I am pleased to say I have this ... escaped the influenza.

With kindest regards
Believe me
Dear Sir
very faithfully yours
Rich Daft.

Part of Daft's correspondence with the publisher of 'Kings of Cricket'.

limited edition signed and numbered by the author as No. 173. The numbers mounted as would-be subscribers approached Richard or Tillotsons. C.J.Britton believed that 300 copies were printed.

That the trade edition, also published in 1893, sold widely – at three shillings and sixpence – is demonstrated by the ease with which copies can still be purchased today. Its cover, originally a deep green, has matured to bluish black. The printing of the text is identical to that of the large-paper limited edition in which the print sits amid wide margins. Both editions contain xiv prelims followed by 274 pages.

Whether Richard could have put the book together without the help of his elder son, Richard Parr Daft, we shall never know. Richard junior had spent years listening to his father's stories, playing all kinds of sport with him, and managing the Radcliffe brewery. We get a glimpse of the relationship between father and sons from *Old Ebor's* piece about Richard in *Talks with Old English Cricketers* published in 1900. Clearly, members of the family were around Richard when the author, A.W.Pullin, interviewed him at home: there is a teasing intervention towards the end when the discussion moved to Richard's continuing career as an active cricketer. He was aged about 63: 'When not umpiring, Richard Daft still plays with and stimulates the Notts Castle team, and not infrequently shows the rising generation the kind of cricket that made him famous.' . . . 'It is the first twenty minutes that trouble me' he says, 'getting my muscles free; my sight is as good as ever it was.'

Old Ebor gathered from another member of the Castle team present (perhaps Richard junior or Harry) that Mr. Daft is a martinet in the field. 'If you miss a catch, you take the first train home rather than face him. If you have got a few runs and look proud, he will tell you, "If some of you fellows get six, you want to wrap them up in a parcel and carry them home." Then when I get wickets with my insignificant bowling, he tells me, "What wretched piffle! It's too bad to hit . . ." but I gather the Castle men venerate their leader!'

The best-known part of *Kings of Cricket* is Andrew Lang's introduction. This wonderful piece of imaginative writing forms, as Lang intended, an elegant gateway to the book, though he is mildly critical of the absence from the reminiscences of much on university cricket – though Richard's association with Oxford and

Cambridge was minimal. Lang refers, nevertheless, to players in those matches whose memories are fragrant and immortal. On this peg he hangs his evocation:

> There is no talk, none so witty and brilliant that is so good as cricket talk, when memory sharpens memory and the dead live again, the regretted, the unforgotten, and the old happy days of burned out Junes revive. We shall not see them again. We lament that lost lightness of heart, 'for no man under the sun lives twice, outliving his day . . . ' Cricket is simply the most catholic and diffused, the most innocent, kindly, and manly of popular pleasures, while it has been the delight of statesmen and the relaxation of learning. There was an old Covenanting minister of the straitest sect, who had so high an opinion of curling that he said if he were to die in the afternoon, he could imagine no better way than curling of passing the morning. Surely we may say as much for cricket. Heaven (as the bishop said of the strawberry) might doubtless have devised a better diversion, but as certainly no better has been invented than that which grew up on the village greens of England.

Then we move into the company of that man who is happy with the world and his place in it. Richard Daft begins: 'I was born at Nottingham on 2 November, 1835 and began to play cricket at a very early age.' Thus, he disposes of antecedents and childhood. The narrative moves into a succession of anecdotes about Old Clarke, and we are out into mid-stream as memories of Fuller Pilch, Alfred Mynn and other great players of Daft's young days hove into view. Many of the incidents and stories about the All England Eleven have been plundered by cricket historians. About William Clarke:

> Clarke played until he was quite an old man; and as he had only one eye (the sight of the other having been destroyed at fives), George Parr used to say that in his latter days he played not by *sight* but by *sound*. The old man was very queer-tempered in these days, too (as I have since found to be the case with most of us cricketers as we grow older), and was consequently a considerable trial to the patience of many of the younger members of his elevens.

> Clarke always put a stop to all 'bragging' on the part of young players with whom he came in contact. One of his sayings, which speaks volumes, I often quote at the present time:

'Fighting in the ring is quite another thing.' This was what Clarke always said to those who often tried to induce him to play young local players in some of his own great matches.

Richard's assessment of George Parr:

> In 1859, George was perhaps now just a trifle past his best, but was still, as he had been for years past, the premier batsman of England. He was a good-looking man, of medium height, and was of a very powerful build. His defence was a little clumsy, as he always played very low down, and was often much punished about the hands in consequence. His hitting all round was terrific. Those who think he could only hit to leg are vastly mistaken, as he could cut and drive almost equally well. All the team, especially we young ones, stood somewhat in awe of him, for George was always rather a queer-tempered man.

The portraits which Richard paints in *Kings of Cricket* are among the best pieces of his writing. Of Arthur Shrewsbury and William Gunn, who followed him in a distinguished line of batsmen for their county, and in turn set up as his rivals in business, he writes with generosity:

> Arthur Shrewsbury began in the way in which I am confident all young players should begin; namely, perfecting himself in his defence first and leaving the hitting to come afterwards. The great secret of Shrewsbury's success has been, without doubt, his marvellous defensive powers. He always knew, I believe, that in this part of his play he most excelled, and cultivated it accordingly. Against Yorkshire, in 1876, he and I put on 183 before the first wicket fell.

and of William Gunn:

> William Gunn played his first match in my last year as a member of the County Eleven. I have always been a great admirer of his play, as, indeed, everyone must be who sees him. He is one of the few big men who make the most of their height and reach. His wrist play is perfect, and his off-hitting brilliant in the extreme.

W.G. and his family were bound to fall under the author's eye:

> I first played against Dr E.M.Grace and his brother Henry at Bath in 1860, but it was a year or two afterwards when Dr E.M.

came into note. His scores were almost always as much talked about as was his brother, Dr W.G., more recently.

I had the pleasure of knowing both the mother and father of this famous player. The former knew ten times more about cricket than any lady I ever met. As an instance of this, I will here mention a circumstance often talked of by George Parr. During the time of the palmy days of the All England Eleven, Mrs Grace wrote to Parr, asking him to play her son (E.M.) in some of his matches, as she was sure, she said, he had the making of a fine player; and said she had a younger son who would in time make a better batsman than any of his brothers, for his *back play* was superior to theirs.

Soon after his appearance amongst us, W.G. rose into the front rank of English batsmen. His astounding feats with the bat could have been accomplished by no man, however good a player, who was not possessed of great physical advantages, an iron constitution, and who did not live temperately. There has never been any show about his play, and it is only the best judges who can most fully appreciate his great abilities. His defence has always been perfect, his hitting powerful and clean, and the way in which he is able to *place* a ball for runs is truly marvellous.

William Caffyn, for whose book *Seventy-one Not Out* Richard junior performed similar editorial services, was also the subject of a short sketch: 'Of William Caffyn's play, I cannot speak too highly. It is a pity such players as he should ever grow old. A superior man in every way was Caffyn. He always dressed well and had a smart and neat appearance at all times.' But, according to Richard, this did not stop some joker from flattening a dead mouse and inserting it in the lining of Caffyn's silk Sunday hat.

Richard regarded the last chapter of *Kings of Cricket* as the most important part of the book and, certainly, Arrowsmith thought sufficiently well of it to publish *Daft's Hints on Cricket* as a separate booklet at the price of six old pennies - 2½ pence.

The technology for action photography had to await the pioneering work of George Beldam early in the next century. Before that time, enthusiasts had to be content with grainy pictures of 'poseurs' or engravings, such as those with which Richard's coaching instructions are illustrated, showing him executing a wide variety of strokes. A certain curiosity attaches to that extinct shot, the draw, of which Richard was one of the last practitioners, by which the batsman places the ball to leg by playing it between the leg stump – and his legs.

Richard concludes his *Hints*: 'Lastly, some cricketers are born and others are made; but anyone ought to make himself a fair player by perseverance.' The conclusion to his penultimate chapter makes a better summation of his career: 'And here I have gone through the whole of my career down to the present time and look back to the time I was a young man; I am far from regretting that I have been a cricketer; and he who has never indulged in this noblest of all pastimes, be he prince or peasant, has missed one of the greatest enjoyments of life.'

Hudson and Kearns made this rather curious attempt in about 1895 to catch Richard Daft's character.

Chapter Twenty-One
Winding Up

In the 1890s, the family's focus shifted onto the football career of Harry, now a professional, with Notts County F.C.[4] In 1893/94, while in Division Two, they defeated Bolton Wanderers 4-1 in the F.A. Cup Final at Goodison Park. There was great rejoicing in Nottingham and the team were photographed with the Cup. As it was stolen a year later, while on display in Birmingham, they were the last holders of the original. In 1897, County returned to Division One. A sign of the times was the appointment during the season of 1894/95 of William Gunn, still only 38 years old and one of the leading batsmen of the age, as a director of the Club.

Richard tells of his visit to The Oval during the season of 1890/91, when Notts County were to play Blackburn Rovers there in the Cup Final:

> Knowing there would be an awful crush in the trains on the day of the match, I decided to go up to London the day previously. On the morning of the match, I soon encountered a large body of men who, from the cards in their hats, I easily discerned were supporters of the famed Lancashire club. . . . I saw many of them eyeing me with great apparent interest, but as I was attired in a tall hat and frock coat, they . . . were rather doubtful of my identity . . . they let me get 15/20 yards past them when one of the party raised the cry at the top of his voice, 'Play up, Notts.' This caused me to turn round quickly, whereupon the Lancastrians immediately gave me a hearty cheer.

These rosy images give no idea how Richard's business life deteriorated in the 1890s. When he gave up the first-class game after the season of 1880, he should have had the edge on Shrewsbury and Gunn, who were still heavily committed to play with Nottinghamshire, but they were young and active men

---

4   Harry also played for Corinthians, the London-based amateur side, from 1887 to 1890. His appearances included a famous match at Richmond-upon-Thames in November, 1889, when the amateurs beat Preston North End 5-0 in the season after the Lancashire club had won both the FA Cup and the League.

devoted to their investment. Things really began to go wrong for Richard in 1888 when Shaw engaged W.J.Bates, who had been the manager of Richard's shop, to supervise the partnership's store. Shrewsbury wrote: 'I hope Bates turns out well. ... Daft had said he would get rid of Bates very soon. If he is a really good man, Daft has acted simple in losing him.' Yet the reason for Daft releasing Bates may have been that Harry Daft, now aged 22, had joined his father in the business. In 1888, Richard's Nottingham shop was described as the 'largest athletic emporium in the world'. The following year, the Shrewsbury partnership closed their Carrington Street Bridge shop, as well as their factory, but they had positive intent as they reopened both sides of their undertaking under a single roof at 6 Queen's Bridge Road. Meanwhile, Richard had widened his interests: as we have seen, after his trip to the United States and Canada, he had opened an agency supplying cricketers of particular skills, even dispatching spin bowlers to India in response to telegrams from maharajahs as well as responding to requests from the States. By September 1888, he had that second shop in Nottingham at St. Peter's Square, where he retailed bags and portmanteaux.

In 1891, Richard found that licensed premises which he occupied were to be sold by auction. They were in the Bingham Road at Radcliffe, and every detail of the house was in the auction particulars – except the name of the inn. Slow retrenchment became the order of the day. On 27 November, 1891 Richard gave up the licence of the Chesterfield Arms. A little more than a year later he closed the business at St Peter's Square on expiry of his lease. Two weeks later, an announcement appeared in the local papers: 'Messrs. R.P. and H.B.Daft beg to inform their friends and the public that their father, Mr. Richard Daft, having given up the business for many years carried on by him at Lister Gate and St. Peter's Square, Nottingham, as a manufacturer of and a dealer in articles connected with cricket and British sports and outfittings, they have commenced business on their own account at Carrington Street Bridge, Nottingham, and hope by strict attention to business and by supplying first-class goods at moderate prices, to merit a share of the support so liberally bestowed upon their father.'

On 3 March 1893, an announcement appeared in the local press that Richard Daft's business had removed from St. Peter's Square to 18a Wheeler Gate, the Central Sports Depot, where the manager was W.J.Bates! His return to Richard was accompanied by an act of treachery, as he took with him a complete list of all Shaw and Shrewsbury's overseas contacts. Before any use could be made of the information, the new venture went bust during the summer. F.H.Ayres, the London sports business, bought out the stock and the lease and kept on Bates as manager – but not for long.

In 1895, Richard borrowed £1,400 from his daughters, Ann, Amy and Mary, to enable him, in partnership with Harry, to take over the Trent Bridge Inn, where he had been involved in the eighties. The combination of the name of Daft and Trent Bridge ought to have been a winner. There must have been countless thousands of young men living on till the 1950s or 60s who later recalled Richard's upright figure and mane of white hair behind the bar, aided and abetted by the roguish, heavily moustached Harry. But their partnership did not last two years before they were advised to cut their losses. They petitioned for their own bankruptcy on 30 November, 1897. It was not for Richard an easy way out. First, it also brought down the sports business which Harry was carrying on in partnership at 85 Carrington Street, Nottingham – Richard junior had resigned a year or two before and Harry had taken in Bernard Barnett – and it could have been disastrous for the Radcliffe Brewery, but as that did not come into the frame as one of his assets, either it was in Mary's name or they must have already closed it down. Second, there was the public examination in bankruptcy to be faced.

The hearing in the Nottingham County Court commenced on 20 January, 1898 with an investigation of the joint failure of Richard and Harry at the Trent Bridge Inn. They had started trading there in March, 1896. By the end they had trade assets of only £127 7s 0d to set against joint liabilities of £3,374 9s 2d – at least £170,000 in modern terms. Richard would have been just about solvent outside of the business, but Harry's debts exceeded his assets by £260 – you could have purchased a decent house for £260 in 1897. They had no capital at all when they took over the inn and so, as already described, had borrowed from Richard's daughters. Their drawings had been double their income; they had spent a considerable sum on 'building up the business' which they expected to get back later. They agreed that they did not see themselves as insolvent. Questioned about how the sum of £1,000 had been spent, one of them responded, 'Of course, there were household expenses at Radcliffe, and a considerable part of it has been spent at Trent Bridge, in our own personal expenses, and in treating customers and expenses of that kind . . . '

'Now, Mr. Daft, I would ask you, has none of this money gone in betting?' reported the paper. They admitted that some has gone at the racecourses, but claimed that losses were not great. There was no evidence that Richard, at any rate, attended more than one race meeting a month. Harry told the court that he received £100 as a professional cricketer, but it had cost him more than half of that to play. He, too, had lost a little at racing. Richard added a description of a real financial tangle: some years before, he had borrowed a sum of money from Messrs Wright, and when that was called in, he borrowed £209 from his two eldest daughters, which they raised from their interest in a will: he had to pay them back before he borrowed the £1,400 from all three daughters. Mrs Daft mortgaged her property at Radcliffe to lend £200 to Richard and Harry.

Daft's old inn is nowadays hemmed in by traffic paraphernalia and overlooked by floodlighting pylons.

Then it was all over. Harry's effects were sold by auction on 12 February, 1898. Mary's property was the only saving grace amid the financial shambles. It is not clear when the brewery perished.

Richard still had friends in the world of cricket, and in March 1898, on the nomination of Notts, he was appointed to the list of first-class umpires. He remained a respected figure in the cricket world: he was one of the great and the good who were asked by the editor of *Wisden*, Sydney Pardon, from time to time to give their views on various problems of the day. A vital issue in the early 1890s was the follow-on. In a two-innings match, the side which batted second and were all out for 80 or more runs behind their opponents had to go in again, and this sometimes resulted in the side which had a great advantage in the first innings having to bat last after the wearisome business of bowling compulsorily in two consecutive innings. Another absurd law provided that a side could not declare their innings closed before the last day of a three day match. In *Wisden* 1894, Richard's view on the follow-on was: 'I think that the follow-on rule should be done away with, now that the declaring rule has come in.' He presumably based his decision on the grounds that if one artificial constraint on a side's tactics was removed, so should the other.

A year later, the complaints about bowlers with unfair deliveries had been increasing. Richard's view was a highly conservative one: 'I saw most of the first-class bowlers last season and although occasionally there might be a ball that was the least bit suspicious, upon the whole I could not, if I had been umpire, have "no-balled" it. I do not think there is anything to complain of regarding our first-class bowlers.' There were, though, undoubted throwers in the first-class game at the time, and Richard was echoing the timid approach of the professional umpires who were not prepared either to wreck a fellow professional's career or to incur the wrath of the county establishments by no-balling an amateur.

Many of his colleagues were distinguished contemporaries from his playing days: these included Bob Carpenter, Dick Barlow, James Lillywhite and Alfred Shaw. Most respected was Bob Thoms, who had been officiating for over thirty years, a true old friend of Richard's who stood in his benefit match back in 1876. None of these officials was highly stretched as there were 35 of them available for selection. In 1898, Thoms umpired only ten first-class matches, Shaw in eight, and Richard in nine, resulting in 22 days of cricket for him.

Early in 1899, Richard had a further opportunity of expressing his views in *Wisden* on one or two features of the previous season, high scoring and the lbw rule, but his response in *Wisden* 1899 was not a very enlightening contribution to the debate!

In 1899, the presence of the Australians, who had a lengthy fixture list, increased the demands on umpires. Richard did not stand in any of their matches but his own list increased to eleven contests. In mid-May, he officiated at Bristol when Wilfred Rhodes returned figures of six wickets for 16 for Yorkshire versus Gloucestershire (without W.G. who had made an acrimonious withdrawal). Rhodes died as recently as 1973 and must have been the last survivor of those who took the field with Richard. This period of Richard's career ended on 26 August, 1899. Surrey were playing Lancashire at The Oval. It was an important match played for the benefit of Tom Richardson, the Surrey and England fast bowler, who in the four English seasons 1894 to 1897 gathered no fewer than 1,005 first-class wickets. Bobby Abel accumulated a score of 178, and Lockwood and Jephson also put together centuries towards Surrey's total of 556, and they went on to defeat Lancashire by an innings. Then Richard returned home for the winter and as full a round of activity as his limited means would allow.

The year 1899 brought distinction to Richard junior when a second book of reminiscences appeared under his editorship. Little is known of the later career of Richard junior. He played three matches for Berkshire in August 1896, with moderate success, but he has no other known connection with the county. The title page called him 'Mid-On' and the volume was *Seventy-One Not Out*, the autobiography of William Caffyn of Surrey, of whom Richard had such a high opinion. Caffyn had a special claim to fame as one who played a distinctive part in the development of the game in Australia when he stayed behind after his second tour there, and became a celebrated coach. This book, too, was a conspicuous success and is full of anecdotes but it lacks the rich texture of *Kings of Cricket*. Richard junior had grown up with his fond parent's tales, and Richard was a more comfortable co-operator than was the silky Caffyn.

On 29 June 1899, Mary and Richard's daughter Ann was married at St. Mary's Church, Radcliffe, to George Frederick Plumpton, a traveller in wines and spirits from Widnes, Lancashire, where the young couple set up home. This was not destined to be a permanent relationship. In December came the death of Richard's eldest surviving brother, John, who was 74. John had attained middle-class respectability as a builder in Nottingham.

Later that winter, Richard's umpiring stint came to an end. He was one of the unlucky ones when the first-class list was drastically

131

reduced from 35 to 20. The explanation given by Lord's was that officials with engagements at schools or colleges for part of the year were excluded – 'it in no way reflected upon the manner in which they had discharged their duties.' Richard had no such engagements. The possibility of his being physically unfit then is rather discounted by the listing of his name under the section headed 'Other Umpires'. At a time when the authorities were looking for umpires to take a firm stance on throwing, maybe his conservative views on the subject counted against him.

In *Talks with Old English Cricketers*, A.W.Pullin wrote that Richard 'is a wonderfully preserved man. It is true his hair is silvered but his cheeks reflect the ruddy glow of perfect health, and his carriage is as erect as if he were re-emerging from the pavilion to make his hundred. Regularity of habit, constant exercise, and moderation in diet and drink are the means by which Daft carries his 65 years so easily. "Every morning," says he, "I use the 7lb dumb-bells before dropping into my cold bath. After the tub, I have a two miles walk in all weathers . . . tennis, cycling; three meals a day. Today I have not an ache or a pain or a rheum about me."'

Unfortunately, by the time these words appeared in print, they were no longer true. During the winter, Richard fell ill and soon took to his bed. For all his devotion to fitness, his heart was feeling the strain of his physical activities, and the disaster of his bankruptcy had added to the stress on his hitherto splendid constitution. By the middle of June his condition had become hopeless.

On 25 June, the local paper reported that he was lying at home seriously ill from 'an affection of the heart, complicated by lung trouble.' From that time on, bulletins were issued almost daily from The Rosery. He lingered on until 18 July, 1900, when his body finally gave up the struggle. It was an appropriate coincidence that Richard's death occurred on W.G's birthday – his fifty-second. Richard was in his sixty-fifth year.

Chapter Twenty-Two
Post Mortem

Richard's death certificate specified the cause of death as 'fatty degeneration of the heart, chronic nephritis and syncope', certified by the long-serving general practitioner in Radcliffe, Dr Campbell. *The Nottingham Express and Journal* carried a detailed and laudatory assessment of his career as cricketer and businessman. On the day of his funeral, 21 July, 1900, the cricket at Trent Bridge, between Notts and Gloucestershire, was suspended during the period of interment, just as it had been for George Parr nine years before. No ladies were present in church in accordance with Richard's request. Richard junior and Harry were the chief mourners, with other family members, who after the service in St Mary's clustered around the grave in the churchyard across the road. Harry Turner, the Secretary, represented the

St Mary's Church, Radcliffe on a summer's day in 2008.

County Cricket Club, with William Oscroft and Alf Shaw prominent among other former cricketers. Many of Richard's old colleagues and adversaries had gone before.

Of figures prominent in Richard's career, Shrewsbury committed suicide in May 1903, Oscroft died two years later, and Shaw early in 1907. J.D.Gorse, fellow villager, member of the Notts County Committee and bankrupt, was in attendance, as was William Wood, Richard's cousin. William Gunn, playing for his county, sent a wreath, so did the Radcliffe-on-Trent Cricket Club. There was a tribute from

Harry's children: 'Grandpa from Dorothy, Katie, Emma and Willie'.

After the funeral, the family were not to be united for long. By the time of the 1901 census, only Mary Daft and Amy, aged 26, were recorded as being at home. Amy's sister, Mary, at 27, was living at Hornsey, in North London, as companion to a commercial clerk, who was aged 48. Harry, his wife and their daughter Dorothy, who was eight, were living with his mother-in-law at Lorne Grove, Radcliffe. Richard junior was recorded at an hotel in Norfolk Street, off the Strand. He was, at 37, still a bachelor, as he remained.

Richard's grave remained unmarked until, at the end of November 1901, a few friends and admirers did the right thing. The subscribers included Earl Manvers, Lord Harris, Lord Belper and William Gunn. The monumental inscription reads: 'A lasting tribute to the memory of a cricketer who in his day and generation had no compeer in the attributes of elegance before the stumps.' The monument was refurbished in November, 2007 after funds were raised to restore it.

Mary survived Richard for nearly twenty years, dying aged 76 on 2 November, 1918. Her end may have been hastened by tragic events in the family of her brother-in-law Charles Daft, who had been the last of the brothers to die in March, 1915 in his eighty-fifth year. He was spared the knowledge of the passing in quick succession of his daughter-in-law, his son and grandson, both also named Charles Frederick. First, the wife of Charles Daft the younger died. He had for many years travelled to Ireland on behalf of a firm of lace manufacturers in Nottingham, and after her death he took his elder son to Ireland for a short holiday. They set out on their return journey on 10 October, 1918. The mail packet in which they were sailing, *R.M.S.Leinster*, was torpedoed by a German U-boat, with the loss of 480 lives. The news soon reached a young sailor, the last remaining member of the family, who had just come home on leave from the war.

In her will, dated 8 May, 1911, Mary left the residue of her estate between four of her children, to the exclusion of Harry. By 1911, he was a cricket coach at Oxford, many of whose first-class matches he umpired. Perhaps he had left wife and children behind at Radcliffe? Ann was now Mrs. Butler, while Amy had wed George Bell, who was the landlord of the Manvers Arms, as well as farming and running a nursery at Radcliffe.

One, at least, of Richard's business interests had survived his bankruptcy because Mary left all her interest in 'the business of marl dealer carried on in partnership with Richard Parr Daft' to him, provided that he pay £20 per annum to his sister, Mary. The business, which dealt in what had been a profitable commodity, had escaped when Richard's financial difficulties had come to a head, perhaps because Mary claimed it as her own. Marl was a much-used top dressing for cricket squares. The business continued in the hands of Richard junior, who, in his will made in 1921, left everything he possessed 'together with my interest in the marl business now being carried on under the name of Richard Daft at Radcliffe-on-Trent, Notts' to his sister, Mary. On his own death in a Croydon nursing home in March 1934, he was described as an insurance clerk who lived in Wallington, Surrey. He had never followed up his early literary success. Butler Parr junior died in the same year, just, on 31 December. In an active life as businessman, sportsman and local councillor, he can never have regretted his decision to keep out of the family brewery at Radcliffe-on-Trent.

The last survivors of Richard's immediate family were Mary and Amy. Mary spent most of her life living quietly in North Wales until her death in 1961, at the age of 85. Harry had died on 10 January, 1945 at High Cross in Hertfordshire. His involvement in cricket continued at Oxford University until 1914 and later as a coach at Haileybury College. He umpired in Oxford University home matches regularly from 1900 to 1914 and missed, by only one year, officiating contemporaneously with his father in first-class cricket. Amy Bell died on 21 February, 1958.

Harry was interviewed by E.V.Lucas in connection with his preparation of *100 Years of Trent Bridge*, which turned out to be his last book published in 1938, the year of his death. Lucas found Harry in Hertfordshire where he had remained after his retirement, living with his daughter and son-in-law. Lucas wrote: 'Harry Daft, whom I used to see in the field and can recall as an inconspicuous, serious player, is now an old gentleman of military cut, with a small white moustache and a merry eye. Of his father – The Governor – he has much to say and cannot over-praise the encouragement to sport of every kind which was given him in his youth ... the talk recurred again and again to The Governor, who was a stern captain but a just one, who enjoyed life in every aspect; who never touched anything until the evening, but then liked his bottle as a man should.' Harry preserved the silver tea and coffee service which was presented to Richard after his testimonial in 1876 and his portrait by Frank Miles. The portrait now hangs in the Long Room at Trent Bridge.

Some years after Richard's death, *The Dictionary of National Biography* did his memory the honour of a contribution: he appears in the 2004 edition, too. In 1923, Ashley-Cooper published his history *Nottinghamshire Cricket and Cricketers* – he had briefly served the county as Secretary in 1921 – in which his sketch of Richard included this:

> At mid-off and long-leg, he was seen to the greatest advantage. He covered much ground, was quick and sure in his movements, and had a long, low, swift and accurate throw-in, the wicket-keeper receiving the ball on the first bound. Many will be able to recall his energies whilst running almost on the toes of the ring, and with his straw hat often blowing off – a pleasant reminiscence which, even at this distance of time, makes one experience a thrill of delight.

Three years later, the visit of the Australians under Herbie Collins in 1926 produced a small flood of cricket books, including several from the publishers Chapman and Hall. They produced *A Cricketer's Yarns*, further cullings from Richard's reminiscences, and not noticeably less interesting than the earlier production. The introduction contained the family lore which Ashley-Cooper obtained from young Richard. They also published Catton's book *Wickets and Goals*. Let him, who had known Richard for so long, have the last word with this assessment:

> While he had the facility to make money, unfortunately he had not the gift of keeping it. In his later years, he acted as an umpire in first-class cricket. There is nothing incompatible with self-respect in accepting such a position, requiring knowledge, capacity and trustworthiness, but it seemed to me rather derogatory to his dignity – because he was a man who had put himself on a pedestal.

Richard Daft's grave in the cemetery at Vicarage Lane, Radcliffe-on-Trent, following its restoration in 2007.

Acknowledgements

As it happens, the publication of this biography marks the 150th anniversary of Richard Daft's first appearance for Nottinghamshire, but to commemorate this was not in my mind when I began this project in 2002. My initial approach was to Chris Walters of the *Nottingham Evening Post*, who suggested I contact Pam Priestland, the historian of Radcliffe-on-Trent, where Daft spent most of his adult life. Pam startled me by pointing out that I was at school with her husband, Neal. This happy coincidence proved an enormous benefit, as they introduced me to the *History of Radcliffe*, which Pam had edited, and the expansive notes on which it was based. They were also very hospitable, and Neal has provided photographs which appear in this book.

My thanks also go to Lord Butler of Brockwell, the former Cabinet Secretary and head of the Civil Service, the great-grandson of Richard Daft, who has provided the preface and taken a constant interest. His cousins, Graham Butler and Juliet Anstey, were also supportive.

I next approached Peter Wynne-Thomas, the archivist of Nottinghamshire County Cricket Club, and a trail-blazer among cricket historians. Over the years he has solved several puzzles for me and made his learning freely available. He has also read the typescript and saved me from error. I am particularly indebted to William Spencer of The National Archives at Kew, who through the good offices of Mike Spurrier, provided details of John Daft's military career; to Dr Neil Young of the Imperial War Museum, who unveiled (to me) of the mystery of the sinking of *R.M.S.Leinster*. Keith Warsop supplied the details of Daft's association with Nottingham Forest Football Club.

My thanks are also due to John Balfour, Kit Bartlett and John Ward for reading the proofs; to the staff of the Local Studies Library in the Central Library at Nottingham and the principal archivist who answered my enquiries over several months; to Peter Redfern of the Nottingham Family History Society; to the British Library's Newspaper Library at Colindale; to Dawn Bradley of Skegness

Library, and to many other county archivists and local studies libraries.

David Jeater has proved to be a patient and knowledgeable editor, while Peter Griffiths, in addition to typesetting the text, completed a long outstanding piece of the jigsaw. Philip Bailey and Gerald Hudd provided valuable statistical help. Roger Mann and Patrick Jeater have assisted with illustrations from their own collections. My thanks, too, to Zahra Ridge for her cover design.

None of this would have been possible without Jean Jones, who typed, typed and typed again the text, after making sense of my scrawl. She and my long-suffering wife, Jill, are two of the five people who are really well informed about Richard Daft.

It gave great pleasure to many people that Richard's grave was refurbished in December, 2007, thanks to Barbara and Stephen Baldwin, and to Pam and Neal Priestland, who spearheaded the fund-raising operation and saw it through to completion.

Neil Jenkinson
Winchester, July 2008

Bibliography

Books and Articles

Viscount Alverstone and C.W.Alcock, *Surrey Cricket: Its History and Associations,* Longmans, 1902

F.S.Ashley-Cooper, *Nottinghamshire Cricket and Cricketers,* Saxton, 1923

[Sir] J.D.Astley, *Fifty Years of My Life in The World of Sport at Home and Abroad,* Hurst and Blackett, 1894

Philip Bailey, Philip Thorn and Peter Wynne-Thomas, *Who's Who of Cricketers* [Second Edition], Hamlyn in association with ACS, 1993

W.A.Bettesworth, *The Walkers of Southgate,* Methuen and Co., 1900

W.A.Bettesworth, *Chats on the Cricket Field,* Merritt and Hatcher, 1910

Gerald Brodribb, *The Lost Art,* Boundary Books, 1997

Edwin Browne, *English Tour to America 1879,* edited notes published in *The Cricket Statistician,* 37, pp17-24; 38, pp 20-22; and 39, pp 29-33, all in 1982

R.W.Brooke and others [eds], *First-Class Cricket Matches 1855-9* [and other years to 1891], ACS Publications, various years

William Caffyn, *Seventy-one Not Out: The Reminiscences of William Caffyn,* Blackwood and Sons, 1899 [Edited by 'Mid On', R.P.Daft]

J.A.H.Catton ['Tityrus'], *Wickets and Goals: Stories of Play,* Chapman and Hall, 1926

Richard Daft, *Kings of Cricket,* Simpkin and Marshall, and Arrowsmith, 1893

Richard Daft and F.S.Ashley-Cooper, *A Cricketer's Yarns,* Chapman and Hall, 1926

David Frith, *The Trailblazers,* Boundary Books, 1999

Edward Grayson, *Corinthians and Cricketers,* Naldrett Press, 1955

Lord Harris, *A Few Short Runs,* Murray, 1921

Arthur Haygarth, *MCC Scores and Biographies: Volumes 5 to 16,* Longmans, various years

Basil Haynes and John Lucas, *The Trent Bridge Battery,* Willow Books, 1985

Brian Heald and others [eds], *The Cricket Season of 1863* [and
    other years to 1880], ACS Publications, various years

Rev R.S.Holmes, *A History of Yorkshire County Cricket
    1830-1903*, Archibald Constable, 1904

Richard Iliffe and Wilfred Baguley, *Victorian Nottingham: A Story
    in Pictures*, Nottingham Historical Film Unit, 1977

T.Horan, *Horan's Diary, Australian Tour, 1877-79*, ACS
    Publications, 2001

Michael Joyce, *Football League Players' Records: 1888-1939*,
    Soccerdata, 2004

Jim Ledbetter, *Nottinghamshire County Cricket Club: 100 Greats*,
    Tempus Publishing Ltd, 2003

D.J.Leighton, *Montague Druitt: Portrait of a Contender*,
    Hydrangea Publishing, 2005

E.V.Lucas [ed], *A Hundred Years of Trent Bridge*, privately
    published, 1938

Patrick Morrah, *Alfred Mynn and the Cricketers of His Time*,
    Constable and Co., 1963

An Old Boy, *Lord's Sixty Years Ago*, in *World of Cricket* magazine,
    August, 1914

Pamela Priestland, *Radcliffe-on-Trent 1837 to 1920*, Ashbracken,
    1989

A.W.Pullin ['Old Ebor'], *Talks with Old English Cricketers*,
    Blackwood and Sons, 1900

R.J.Reynolds, *The Conduct of Matches in the 19th Century*, in *The
    Cricket Statistician*, 119, pp 26-29

Simon Rae, *W.G.Grace: A Life*, Faber and Faber, 1998

Ric Sissons, *The Players: A Social History of the Professional
    Cricketer*, The Kingswood Press, 1988

Wray Vamplugh, *Pay Up and Play the Game*, Cambridge
    University Press, 1988

Keith Warsop, *Historical Research versus Football Tradition: The
    Formation of Notts County*, in *Soccer History*, 1, 2002

Tony Webb [ed], *The Minor Counties Championship 1896*, ACS
    Publications, 2005

J.R.Webber, *The Chronicle of W.G.*, ACS Publications, 1998

G.Derek West, *The Elevens of England*, Darf Publishers, 1988

Peter Wynne-Thomas, *Nottinghamshire Cricketers 1821-1914*,
    Author, 1971

Peter Wynne-Thomas, *Give Me Arthur: a biography of Arthur
    Shrewsbury*, Arthur Barker, 1986

Peter Wynne-Thomas, *George Parr: His Record Innings by Innings*, ACS Publications, 1993

Peter Wynne-Thomas, *Nottinghamshire CCC First Class Records 1826-1995*, Limlow Books, 1996

Peter Wynne-Thomas, *150 Years of Trent Bridge*, Nottinghamshire County Cricket Club, 1998

Other publications

Baily's Magazine of 1891

Bell's Life in London in various years

Census returns for 1841 to 1901

Cricket magazine in 1886, 1891 and 1900

The Dictionary of National Biography, including its supplementary volumes

Fores's Sporting Notes in 1891

James Lillywhite's Cricketers' Annual from 1872 to 1899

John Lillywhite's Cricketers' Companion from 1865 to 1882

The Times newspaper in various years

Wisden's Cricketers' Almanack from 1864 to 1901

Appendix One
Some Statistics

The statistical details given below relate to Richard Daft's performances in matches identified as first-class by the Association of Cricket Statisticians and Historians and listed in its 1996 publication *Complete First-Class Match List: Volume 1, 1801-1914.*

First-Class cricket: Batting and Fielding

	M	I	NO	R	HS	Ave	100	50	Ct
1858	8	16	3	210	44*	16.15	-	-	10
1859	7	14	2	223	52	18.58	-	1	6
1860	13	22	1	380	44	18.09	-	-	14
1861	14	26	0	584	66	22.46	-	4	9
1862	10	15	2	346	118	26.61	1	-	9
1863	5	9	1	231	80*	28.87	-	1	5
1864	11	20	1	498	80	26.21	-	4	8
1865	7	12	1	359	78	32.63	-	4	8
1866	7	13	1	255	94	21.25	-	2	3
1867	6	12	5	377	111*	53.85	1	2	3
1868	7	13	0	335	94	25.76	-	3	5
1869	9	14	4	494	103*	49.40	1	3	4
1870	9	15	4	565	117	51.36	1	3	4
1871	12	19	4	565	92	37.66	-	6	11
1872	13	20	3	589	102	34.64	1	4	9
1873	8	12	2	416	161	41.60	1	1	7
1874	12	21	0	453	102	21.57	1	-	8
1875	14	23	2	354	47	16.85	-	-	4
1876	18	30	2	976	99	34.85	-	6	6
1877	15	30	2	699	96	24.96	-	3	4
1878	17	25	1	403	69*	16.79	-	2	8
1879	11	19	2	174	52	10.23	-	1	6
1880	14	22	3	237	47	12.47	-	-	4
1881	2	3	0	13	7	4.33	-	-	-
1883	2	2	0	25	23	12.50	-	-	-
1891	3	4	0	27	13	6.75	-	-	-
Career	**254**	**431**	**46**	**9788**	**161**	**25.42**	**7**	**50**	**155**

Notes: Daft played all his first-class cricket in England. Between 1860 and 1880, batsmen were dismissed in most English seasons at an average of between 15 and 18 runs per wicket. In his career as a whole, Daft was dismissed 191 times caught (50%), 131 times bowled (34%), 23 times run out (6%), 18 times stumped (5%), 13 times lbw (3%) and nine times hit wicket (2%). He retired hurt twice. The three bowlers who took his wicket most often were W.G.Grace 23, W.Caffyn 18 and T.Emmett 16. Daft played 157 matches for Nottinghamshire, scoring 6,627 runs at 29.32 and taking 92 catches.

First-Class cricket: Bowling

	O	M	R	W	BB	Ave	5i
1858	19.3	1	63	4	2-14	15.75	-
1864	35	11	51	2	2-36	25.50	-
1866	4	2	17	0	-	-	-
1869	36.2	9	72	8	5-23	9.00	1
1870	56	12	122	5	3-29	24.40	-
1871	26	4	73	0	-	-	-
1872	96	22	217	15	6-59	14.46	1
1873	20	6	40	2	2-24	20.00	-
1875	10.3	0	32	1	1-7	32.00	-
1876	9	0	35	0	-	-	-
1877	166	50	290	13	3-39	22.30	-
1878	6	0	15	0	-	-	-
1883	18	4	43	1	1-24	43.00	-
Career	**503**	**121**	**1070**	**51**	**6-59**	**20.98**	**2**

Notes: Overs were of four balls throughout Daft's career as a bowler. He took his wickets at the rate of one per 39.45 balls and conceded runs at the rate of 2.12 per four-ball over. Daft took wickets in 23 matches: 24 (47%) of his wickets were caught, including two caught and bowled; 15 (29%) were bowled; 11 (22%) an exceptional proportion, were stumped and one (2%) was lbw. For Nottinghamshire he took 45 wickets at 18.64. He took the wickets of seven batsmen twice; all his other victims were once only.

First-class cricket: Fifties (57)

Score	For	Opponent	Venue	Season
52	Nottinghamshire[1]	Surrey	The Oval	1859
65	Players[1]	Gentlemen	Lord's	1861
66	All England Eleven[2]	United England Eleven	Old Trafford	1861
64	North[1]	Surrey	The Oval	1861
55	England[2]	Kent	Canterbury	1861
118	North[1]	South	Lord's	1862
80*	Nottinghamshire[2]	Kent	Trent Bridge	1863
61	Players[1]	Gentlemen	The Oval	1864
56	Nottinghamshire[1]	Surrey	The Oval	1864
78	Nottinghamshire[2]	Kent	Crystal Palace	1864
80	Nottinghamshire[1]	Yorkshire	Bradford (Gt Horton Rd) 1864	
67	Nottinghamshire[1]	Sussex	Trent Bridge	1865
78	North[1]	South	Lord's	1865
52*	Nottinghamshire[2]	Surrey	Trent Bridge	1865
66	Nottinghamshire[1]	Yorkshire	Bradford (Gt Horton Rd) 1865	
52	Nottinghamshire[1]	Cambridgeshire	Trent Bridge	1866
94	Nottinghamshire[2]	Middlesex	Islington	1866
111*	All England Eleven[1]	United England Eleven	Old Trafford	1867
72*	Nottinghamshire[1]	Middlesex	Islington	1867
62*	Nottinghamshire[2]	Cambridgeshire	Trent Bridge	1867
94	Nottinghamshire[1]	Lancashire	Trent Bridge	1868
57	Nottinghamshire[2]	Surrey	The Oval	1868
51	Nottinghamshire[1]	Yorkshire	Dewsbury	1868
103*	Nottinghamshire[2]	MCC	Lord's	1869
56	Nottinghamshire[1]	Surrey	Trent Bridge	1869
93*	Nottinghamshire[1]	Surrey	The Oval	1869
50	Nottinghamshire[1]	Yorkshire	Sheffield (Bramall Lane) 1869	

55	Nottinghamshire[1]	Surrey	The Oval	1870
80	Nottinghamshire[2]	Surrey	The Oval	1870
117	Nottinghamshire[1]	MCC	Lord's	1870
53	Nottinghamshire[2]	MCC	Lord's	1870
50*	Nottinghamshire[2]	Yorkshire	Trent Bridge	1871
68*	Players[2]	Gentlemen	The Oval	1871
68*	Nottinghamshire[1]	Surrey	Trent Bridge	1871
51*	Nottinghamshire[2]	Gloucestershire	Bristol (Clifton College)	1871
92	Nottinghamshire[1]	Surrey	The Oval	1871
84	Nottinghamshire[1]	Gloucestershire	Trent Bridge	1871
102	Players[2]	Gentlemen	Lord's	1872
84	Nottinghamshire[1]	Gloucestershire	Trent Bridge	1872
64	North[1]	South	Canterbury	1872
78	Nottinghamshire[1]	Surrey	The Oval	1872
92*	Nottinghamshire[1]	Gloucestershire	Bristol (Clifton College)	1872
161	Nottinghamshire[1]	Yorkshire	Trent Bridge	1873
56	Nottinghamshire[2]	Surrey	The Oval	1873
102	Nottinghamshire[1]	Sussex	Trent Bridge	1874
70	Nottinghamshire[1]	Lancashire	Trent Bridge	1876
81	Nottinghamshire[1]	Yorkshire	Trent Bridge	1876
61	Players[2]	Gentlemen	The Oval	1876
82	Nottinghamshire[1]	Middlesex	Chelsea (Prince's)	1876
62	Nottinghamshire[2]	Gloucestershire	Bristol (Clifton College)	1876
99	Nottinghamshire[1]	Middlesex	Trent Bridge	1876
64	Players[1]	Gentlemen	Lord's	1877
96	Nottinghamshire[1]	Middlesex	Lord's	1877
53	Nottinghamshire[2]	Yorkshire	Sheffield (Bramall Lane)	1877
52	Nottinghamshire[1]	Kent	Town Malling	1878
69*	Nottinghamshire[2]	Derbyshire	Trent Bridge	1878
52	Nottinghamshire[1]	Yorkshire	Trent Bridge	1879

First-Class cricket: Five wickets or more in an innings (2)

Bowling	For	Opponent	Venue	Season
14.2-4-23-5	Nottinghamshire	Surrey[2]	The Oval	1869
37-11-59-6	Nottinghamshire	Yorkshire[2]	Sheffield (Bramall Lane)	1872

The index figures [1] and [2] in the two tables immediately above indicate the innings in which the feat was achieved.

Sources for all four tables: First Class Cricket Matches, various years; and www.cricketarchive.com

Appendix Two
Benefit Match Scorecard

NORTH v SOUTH
Played at Trent Bridge, Nottingham, July 17, 18, 19, 1876.
South won by eight wickets.

NORTH

1	A.N.Hornby	c Butler b Southerton	6	b W.G.Grace	44
2	R.Daft	b G.F.Grace	9	run out	38
3	R.P.Smith	b G.F.Grace	18	c Pooley b G.F.Grace	39
4	W.Oscroft	c and b G.F.Grace	27	b Gilbert	0
5	E.Lockwood	run out	0	not out	57
6	A.Greenwood	c Pooley b G.F.Grace	2	c Pooley b G.F.Grace	3
7	G.Ulyett	c Pooley b G.F.Grace	22	c Pooley b Southerton	23
8	A.Shaw	not out	7	c Humphrey b Southerton	0
9	A.Hill	b G.F.Grace	4	c Pooley b Southerton	9
10	†G.Pinder	c and b G.F.Grace	0	c Butler b Southerton	20
11	F.Morley	b G.F.Grace	3	b Southerton	2
	Extras	b 3, lb 1	4	lb 6, w 1	7
	Total		102		242

FoW (1): 1-8, 2-23, 3-43, 4-43, 5-50, 6-79, 7-88, 8-91, 9-91, 10-102
FoW (2): 1-51, 2-126, 3-126, 4-128, 5-136, 6-191, 7-191, 8-205, 9-239, 10-242

SOUTH

1	W.G.Grace	b Shaw	16	not out	114
2	I.D.Walker	c Pinder b Hill	4	(3) b Shaw	20
3	A.J.Webbe	run out	3	(2) c Shaw b Hill	41
4	H.Jupp	c Pinder b Hill	24		
5	W.R.Gilbert	b Shaw	9		
6	G.F.Grace	c Hill b Shaw	1	(4) not out	10
7	†E.W.Pooley	not out	49		
8	R.Butler	c Ulyett b Shaw	20		
9	R.Humphrey	b Hill	11		
10	W.T.Palmer	b Hill	5		
11	J.Southerton	c Lockwood b Shaw	4		
	Extras	b 4, lb 5	9	b 1, nb 4	5
	Total		155	(2 wickets)	190

FoW (1): 1-16, 2-24, 3-26, 4-46, 5-58, 6-76, 7-112, 8-140, 9-148, 10-155
FoW (2): 1-101, 2-157

South Bowling

	O	M	R	W			O	M	R	W
G.F.Grace	30	7	67	8			34	10	82	2
Southerton	29	17	31	1			33.2	16	58	5
W.G.Grace					(3)		26	10	58	1
Gilbert					(4)		24	9	37	1

North Bowling

	O	M	R	W			O	M	R	W
Shaw	98.3	74	50	5			37	21	56	1
Hill	61	35	60	4			27	10	52	1
Morley	23	13	21	0			14	2	36	0
Ulyett	14	9	15	0			10.1	2	30	0
Lockwood					(5)		4	0	11	0

Umpires: R.A.Thoms and R.C.Tinley.   Toss: North

Close of Play: 1st day: South (1) 64-5 (Jupp 23*, Pooley 4*); 2nd day: North (2) 143-5 (Lockwood 9*, Ulyett 3*).

Source: cricketarchive.com

Note: Robert Butler, appearing for the South, was a nephew of George Parr and had been an occasional player for Notts, but was living in London in 1876.